Retrospect: War and Change in
Europe 1914–1955

A note for the general reader

Total War and Social Change: Europe 1914–1955 is the latest honours-level history course to be produced by the Open University. War and Society has always been a subject of special interest and expertise in the Open University's History Department. The appeal for the general reader is that the five books in the series, taken together or singly, consist of authoritative, up-to-date discussions of the various aspects of war and society in the twentieth century.

The books provide insights into the modes of teaching and communication, including the use of audio-visual material, which have been pioneered at the Open University. Readers will find that they are encouraged to participate in a series of 'tutorials in print', an effective way to achieve a complete command of the material. As in any serious study of a historical topic, there are many suggestions for further reading, including references to a Course Reader, set book and to two collections of primary sources which accompany the series. It is possible to grasp the basic outlines of the topics discussed without turning to these books, but obviously serious students will wish to follow up what is, in effect a very carefully designed course of guided reading, and discussion and analysis of that reading. The first unit in Book 1 sets out the aims and scope of the course.

Open University students are provided with supplementary material, including a *Course Guide* which gives information on student assignments, summer school, the use of video cassettes, and so on.

Total War and Social Change: Europe 1914–1955

Book 1 *Europe in 1914*
Book 2 *The Impact of World War I*
Book 3 *Between Two Wars*
Book 4 *The Impact of World War II*
Book 5 *Retrospect: War and Change in Europe 1914–1955*

Other material associated with the course

Primary Sources 1: World War I, eds Arthur Marwick and Wendy Simpson, Open University, 2000

Primary Sources 2: Interwar and World War II, eds Arthur Marwick and Wendy Simpson, Open University, 2000

Secondary Sources, eds Arthur Marwick and Wendy Simpson, Open University, 2000

Total War and Historical Change: Europe 1914–1955, eds. Clive Emsley, Arthur Marwick and Wendy Simpson, Open University Press, 2000 (Course Reader)

J. M. Roberts, *Europe 1880–1945*, Longman, 2001 (third edition) (Set Book)

The Open University

book 5

Retrospect: War and Change in Europe 1914–1955

Arthur Marwick, Bernard Waites, Antony Lentin, Annika Mombauer, Bill Purdue, Mark Pittaway and Clive Emsley

Total War and Social Change: Europe 1914–1955

This publication forms part of an Open University course: AA312 *Total War And Social Change: Europe 1914–1955*. Details of this and other Open University courses can be obtained from the Course Reservations Centre, PO Box 724, The Open University, Milton Keynes MK7 6ZS, United Kingdom: tel. +44 (0)1908 653231, e-mail ces-gen@open.ac.uk

Alternatively, you may visit the Open University website at http://www.open.ac.uk where you can learn more about the wide range of courses and packs offered at all levels by the Open University.

For availability of this or other components, contact Open University Worldwide Ltd, The Berrill Building, Walton Hall, Milton Keynes MK7 6AA, United Kingdom: tel. +44 (0)1908 858785; fax +44 (0)1908 858787; e-mail ouwenq@open.ac.uk; website http://www.ouw.co.uk

The Open University, Walton Hall, Milton Keynes, MK7 6AA

First published 2001 by The Open University. Reprinted 2007

Edited, designed and typeset by The Open University

Printed and bound in the United Kingdom by The Alden Group, Oxford

ISBN 0 7492 85583

Cover illustration: D. S. Moor, *You – Have you Enrolled as a Volunteer Yet?*, 1920, Novosti, London.

1.3

B/AA312_b5_e1i3_N0749285583

MIX
Paper from
responsible sources
FSC® C022612
www.fsc.org

The paper used for this book is FSC-certified and totally chlorine-free. FSC (the Forest Stewardship Council) is an international network to promote responsible management of the world's forests.

CONTENTS

Acknowledgements

Grateful acknowledgement is made to the following sources for permission to use material in this book:

Tables

Table 28.2: Gattrell, P. and Harrison, M. (1992) 'World War II: cumulative military mobilisation and demographic losses of Germany and USSR', *The Russian and Soviet Economies in Two World Wars: A Comparative View*, Basil Blackwell Limited; *Figure 28.5*: Barber, J. and Harrison, M. (1991) 'Soviet employment by branch of output, 1940–5', *The Soviet Home Front, 1941–1945: A Social and Economic History of the USSR in World War II*, © Longman Group UK Limited 1992. Reprinted by permission of Pearson Education Limited; *Table 28.6*: Harrison, M. (ed.) (1998) 'War production of the great powers; the military burden; the net output of German industry', *The Economics of World War II: Six Great Powers in International Comparisons*, Cambridge University Press. *Table 29.2*: Halsey, A. H. (1972) 'Table 4.4', *Trends in British Society since 1900*, Macmillan; *Table 29.3*: Routh, G. (1965) *Occupation and Pay in Great Britain 1906–1960*, Cambridge University Press.

Every effort has been made to trace all the copyright owners, but if any has been inadvertently overlooked, the publishers will be pleased to make the necessary arrangements at the first opportunity.

Unit 28 THE NATURE AND CAUSES OF WAR

ARTHUR MARWICK, BERNARD WAITES, ANTONY LENTIN
AND ANNIKA MOMBAUER

(Introduction by Arthur Marwick; section 1 by Bernard Waites; section 2 by Antony Lentin, Annika Mombauer and Bernard Waites; section 3 by Annika Mombauer)

Open University students of this unit will need to refer to:

Set book: J. M. Roberts, *Europe 1880–1945*, Longman, 2001

Primary Sources 2: Interwar and World War II, eds Arthur Marwick and Wendy Simpson, Open University, 2001

Course Reader: *Total War and Historical Change: Europe 1914–1955*, eds Clive Emsley, Arthur Marwick and Wendy Simpson, Open University Press, 2000

INTRODUCTION

This book, consisting of three units, offers an overview of some of the most important issues relating to total war and social change between 1914 and 1955: a summary and distillation of what has been contained in Books 1–4, with references to books published since those books were written. For students of AA312 this book has the essential purpose of helping them to revise for their exam. But it should also be of interest more generally as a demonstration of how to start thinking about major historical topics.

The crucial point I want to make here is that historical study is concerned with *thinking* almost as much as it is concerned, inevitably, with the accumulation of information, ideas and interpretations. To students preparing for an exam, the advice is: don't try to cram in new information, but instead *refresh* your memory of what you have already learnt, and *reflect* on the sorts of problems and questions you are now expected to be able to address in an informed and intelligent way. I have long argued that whatever the reading, one concentrates more, and therefore retains more, with a number of questions in mind as one reads (good books, of course, will raise new questions of their own). This book contains a series of topics ('revision topics', you could call them, if that does not seem too limiting), all of which could be discussed on the basis of material and ideas already provided in the first four books of the course, though here some fresh perspectives will be opened up. (In fact, a very good way of revising is to look at 'old' material in a slightly 'new' way.) As in other academic subjects, knowledge in history is constantly being extended and refined: the true student of history looks out for new books in the fields in which he or she is interested (through reviews in *The Sunday Times* or *The Times Literary Supplement*, for instance). Earlier books in this course have stressed that many of the biggest issues are open to varying interpretations, so there is no question of our discussions suddenly becoming outdated in the light of new publications. Still, students of total war and social change should want to know if some striking new contribution on the subject is published. (Open University students are supplied with an occasional *Newsletter* which conveys up-to-date bibliographical information.) In Book 5 the opportunity will be taken to relate striking new publications to issues which have been thoroughly discussed.

For students who wish to go back and revise particular topics, this book will endeavour to provide a guide to where, in earlier books of the course, particular issues are discussed. But the course as a whole consists of far more than just the five books (including this one) of structured teaching material. There are video-cassettes, audio-cassettes, a Course Reader, a volume of article- or chapter-length *Secondary Sources*, a *Maps Booklet*, two volumes of *Primary Sources* and a set textbook by J. M. Roberts. Students of history need to demonstrate skills of presenting balanced and well-supported arguments: such arguments should draw upon all the resources available, and Book 5 seeks to exemplify how this should be done.

Some of the revision material may bring out differences of approach among course team members. There *are* differences of approach and, far from trying to conceal this, the course has openly recognized such differences. The authors of this final book are not going to tell you that what a colleague wrote was 'wrong': what judgements you finally come to are up to you. But if you are stimulated to *think* more deeply, that is all to the good. 'Unfair', some students cry. 'How can we decide what to believe if even members of the same course team sometimes disagree? How can different perspectives possibly help us when what we want are certainties with which to approach the exam?' Three answers:

1   Though there may be differences of interpretation or approach, there are no differences about the need to argue *rigorously*, and to base arguments on evidence. It is vital that at this stage you should be completely clear about the basic principles of historical study.

2   In fact, a great deal of historical knowledge on twentieth-century Europe is secure and not subject to serious debate. At this stage, it is very important to be sure about what *can* be taken as soundly established information and interpretation.

3   Above all, the ideal state to have reached towards the end of a history course is that of thinking like a historian: to be positive where it is proper to be positive; to be aware of differences of interpretation where such differences are soundly based; to be cautious without forever sitting on the fence; to be sceptical, but not cynical.

The basic activity of practically all academic endeavour is the solving of problems. In essence, an exam invites you to join in that activity. If there are different views worthy of being cited (this very much depends on the nature of the question), by all means cite them: but do arrive at a conclusion of your own. If you argue well, and produce such evidence as has been made available to you, then it will matter not a bit that the examiner would, personally, have arrived at a different conclusion.

At this point, students of the course should refer to Book 1, Unit 1. Read again the opening section, 'The course title explained', and note the six aims of the course set out on pages 5–39. If the course has been successful, you should now feel that you can meet the course's aims. Book 5 sets out to provide detailed help and reinforcement for particular topics encompassed within the six aims. It would be a good idea now to turn to the end of Unit 1, 'Conclusion: three themes'. Rereading this should help to alert you to the kinds of problems and interrelationships you should be thinking about by this stage of the course.

In introducing Book 5 I should like to suggest that it forms the summing up of the entire *spirit* in which AA312 has been offered. There has been no attempt to insist that war is the most significant agent of change in the twentieth century, or even to insist that war is an important agent of change. The reasons for focusing on war are: (a) that without doubt the two total wars are unavoidable factual phenomena in twentieth-century European history which, whatever their long-term significance, have touched off much argument and debate among historians; and (b) to force you to think about historical explanation, about processes of change and how they are caused. If you believe that structural, ideological and institutional factors are far more important than wars, or that it is the decisions of politicians and political parties which really count, then that is fine by us. The important point is that you should arrive at some thoughts on these matters fundamental to the study of history, rather than just seeing history as a vast array of miscellaneous information. If, in some of the individual sections that follow, it is suggested that other factors are in fact much more important than war, do not despair: this course has not so much been about war, as about the *arguments* (pro and con) over the effects of war, set against the many other possible sources of change.

Now, in my view, the best way to prepare for the exam is to reflect on the *spirit* of AA312. You need factual information, of course, in order to back up your arguments in your exam answers, and to show that you are taking a balanced, not a selective, one-sided approach. And since we recognize that you can't possibly hold in your head all the detailed information you would need to answer every question in the exam paper, and in fact give you a generous choice, you can be selective in what you thoroughly revise for the exam: pick the themes and topics which particularly interest you, making sure that you study them with respect to at least three countries *apart* from Britain, and across the entire chronological span of the course. I'd say that you need, for Parts II and III of the exam, to master detailed content for about half of the course. Think carefully about the advice you have been given in TMA 04 and at Residential School on *thematic* questions. But, having said all that, let me take you back to the spirit of the course. Try to keep in your head the whole framework of the course: try to be in the position that that you could at least write a few sentences on all the major issues relating to war that are raised in the course. Don't try to spot precise exam questions and first prepare answers to them. Remember you have to answer the question that is actually asked, not the one you have mugged up. The exam is not in any way designed to trap you; on the contrary it is designed to enable you to show off what you know *with respect to the issues of this course*. Central is the significance, or absence of it, of *war*. So don't bank on there being a question solely focused on, say, women – we might, for example, set a question focusing on *all* underprivileged groups, or one asking you to contrast the experiences of women with those of men. We want to give you the opportunity to show that you can *think* as well as regurgitate information, and that you can make comparisons and contrasts. What happened in the past is very important. When you are revising keep reflecting on the *significance* of the issues you are studying.

One assumption that is fundamental to all historical study is the critical analysis of primary sources. As you know, you will be asked in Part I of the exam to write commentaries on two extracts from the documents contained in your two volumes of primary sources. The first point is to be absolutely sure you are clear what you are being asked to do: the question asks you to say what the document is, to set it in its historical context, to comment on points in the text, and to sum up its significance for the study of total war and social change. Be very sure that that is exactly what you do. Don't, for instance, write a general essay vaguely related to the subject matter of the extract. You may remember the exercises on primary sources I set in the 'Introduction to History', Parts 1 and 2 in the Level 1 course A103 *Introduction to the Humanities*: there the exercise was almost exclusively in technique and did not call for detailed historical knowledge. In this course, in addition to adopting the correct technique (that is to say, doing exactly what you are asked to do), you need to have a considerable amount of historical knowledge in order to give the historical context, and in order to be able to sum up the significance of the extract. The exercise is designed to bring you as close as possible to the actual practices of a working historian, though, of course, there is inevitably something artificial about it. Historians work from whole documents, and indeed from whole bundles of documents, not from single extracts. We have preselected documents for you, with a clear idea in our own minds of their historical significance. Working historians would seldom be likely to accept the testimony of one single document without checking it against others. You have to take it on trust if we tell you that a particular document is in fact representative of a number of similar documents. The best way of ensuring that you have the right technique for writing commentaries on documents is to: (a) look back to the first TMA on documents that you did and to the comments your tutor made on it; and (b) look back to those places in the course where you were given a very full example of how to do this kind of exercise (Book 1, Unit 1, pp.14–20; Unit 5, pp.182–3; Book 4, Units 21–25, pp.160–4). In a moment, I will talk you through just one more example.

What other advice can I give you about preparing to cope with this aspect of the exam? In the exam you have a choice of two extracts out of six. This suggests that it would be wise to prepare yourself thoroughly on at least half the total number of documents. If you have been working systematically through the course, following our directions, you will already have encountered almost all of the documents; some you may have made use of in your TMAs. The documents are an astonishingly rich and varied collection, which can be read for enlightenment and pleasure. I recommend that you look through both volumes of primary sources trying to see if, at least in a general way, you know why we have chosen each particular document – that is to say, what its significance is. The documents to revise most thoroughly are the ones that fall within subject areas that particularly interest you. It is important that you are familiar with the entire content of these documents: in the exam, you just get a short extract, but in order to be able to comment effectively on it you have to know what is in the rest of the document. (Don't misunderstand me here: in commenting on the extract you refer to the extract in front of you, but, nevertheless, to do this effectively you will nearly always have to make some reference to what else is in the whole document, or about where in the document the extract you are commenting on comes from.) In the 'Introduction to History' (and also in my book *The New Nature of History: Knowledge, Evidence, Language*, 2001), I spell out all the individual critical questions a historian asks of a primary source: we now take for granted that you know you should be looking out for questions of dating, of how biased, or how representative, the author of a particular document is, and so on.

The following extract is similar to one you might encounter in Part I of the exam:

> During the many years of peaceable neighbourly existence, the two countries have become united by many ties, and a social upheaval in the one is bound to affect the other. That these troubles will be of a social, and not a political, nature cannot be doubted, and this will hold true, not only as regards Russia, but for Germany as well. An especially favourable soil for social upheavals is found in Russia, where the masses undoubtedly profess, unconsciously, the principles of Socialism. In spite of the spirit of antagonism to the Government in Russian society, as unconscious as the Socialism of the broad masses of the people, a political revolution is not possible in Russia, and any revolutionary movement inevitably must degenerate into a Socialist movement. The opponents of the government

have no popular support. The people see no difference between a government official and an intellectual. The Russian masses, whether workmen or peasants, are not looking for political rights, which they neither want nor comprehend.

(P. N. Durnovo, memorandum to the Tsar, February 1914)

Now, what I suggest you do (something you couldn't do in the exam, of course!) is turn to the entire document in *Primary Sources 2: Interwar and World War II* (Document II.54). (In fact, this is not the entire document, but extracts from it chosen by the course team.) You will see there that we give you some important information about Durnovo (we generally only do this where such information is not readily available to you in the course units or in Roberts). I suggest that you now read carefully everything that we have printed about Durnovo's memorandum.

As you will have noted, this is an immensely rich document, covering both foreign and domestic issues. Thus, while the general significance of whatever extract you are given to comment on might be roughly the same, its particular significance will depend upon the particular extract in front of you. But you will see also how the extract I have selected takes on much more meaning once you are aware of how it fits in to the memorandum as a whole. Thus, ideally, you should bring with you into the exam room, locked away in your mind (with respect, that is, to dealing with this particular extract), a broad knowledge of all the selections from the memorandum that we have printed for you, the knowledge provided about Durnovo, relevant information about previous developments in Russia from Book 1, Units 2–4, about the origins of the war from Book 1, Unit 5, and about subsequent developments in Russia from Book 2, Units 11–13. You should be able to make use of that knowledge in at least one essay question.

Let us look at the individual questions you have to answer.

What is the document?

To repeat that it is a 'memorandum' doesn't take us much further, but it is still worth stating clearly what the document is. You could then say that it is a piece of private advice being offered to the Tsar by an elder statesman, someone who is (and this is important) representative of the extreme reactionary elements in Russia, who were, of course, both numerous and influential among the upper classes.

What is the document's historical context?

Here the date is clearly of crucial importance. This is seven months before the outbreak of World War I, six months before the fateful assassination of Archduke Franz Ferdinand. The context is one of an international alliance system which has been lining up the powers in two armed camps, and of a series of international crises which, to a right-wing politician like Durnovo, suggested that general war was imminent. He would, of course, be particularly sensitive to the implications of the Balkan Wars. The precise element which has provoked Durnovo's memorandum is the way in which Russia has become embroiled (as he sees it) in an alliance with Britain and France, which puts it in the opposite camp from Germany and means that, if war breaks out (which he believes to be very likely), Russia will be forced to fight against Germany. The purpose of the memorandum is to persuade the Tsar to reverse this policy before it is too late. Essentially the document as a whole consists of a range of arguments in support of this plea. Durnovo's fundamental conviction is that, because of their economic rivalry, war between Germany and Britain is inevitable (interesting how this extreme reactionary presents arguments which are also vintage Marxism!), and that many other powers will then automatically be drawn in to an immensely destructive war. His basic point is that, as the two great conservative powers, Russia and Germany are natural allies. (These two sentences are good examples of contextual points which are derived from knowledge of the entire document.)

Where are the specific points in the text?

The first phrases which call for discussion are 'peaceable neighbourly existence' and 'united by many ties'. Again we find explanations earlier in the document: there is the point about Russia and Germany being the two leading conservative, autocratic and imperial powers, but more important with regard to the second phrase is the question of heavy German investment in Russian industry. From more general historical knowledge, one might comment that the phrase 'peaceable neighbourly existence' is not entirely accurate: under Bismarck it had been a principle of German policy never to come into conflict with Russia, but 'Germany's drive to the east', as seen, for example, in its investment in Turkey, was a potential cause of friction with Russia, and, still more, its support for Austria meant an embroilment in a sharp conflict of interests in the Balkans. The whole sentence forms an important link in Durnovo's argument against Russia becoming involved in a general European war. He argues in the previous paragraph that defeat in such a war would entail social revolution, and he then reasons that because of the close links between the two countries, social upheaval in the one would inevitably lead to social upheaval in the other – thus, even if victory might be envisaged, it still would not be worth becoming embroiled in a war.

The distinction Durnovo makes between 'social' and 'political' is interesting and revealing: what he means becomes clear only once one has read the whole paragraph. It becomes clear that by 'political revolution' he simply means a change in the ruling group; what he means by 'social revolution' becomes fully clear from the beginning of the paragraph that immediately follows our extract (yet another example of the advantages of knowing the document as a whole); social revolution means the peasants gaining land, the workers taking over the capitalist profits of the bosses. The tenor of Durnovo's argument, then, is that the result of war will be much worse than mere political change; it will be complete social upheaval. The soil, he goes on to say, is especially favourable in Russia. There were, of course, developed socialist parties in Russia at this time, particularly the Bolsheviks led by Lenin; but this 'unconscious' socialism that he speaks of seems to be akin to what is often spoken of as the 'land hunger' of the peasants. Undoubtedly that existed.

Durnovo goes on to show his contempt for the political opposition in Russia (presumably he is thinking of the Kadets) who have failed to make the spirit of antagonism to the government conscious. Even more interesting in this sentence is the apparent contrast between Russian society, which he seems to be limiting to those who have some feelings about the nature of government, and the broad masses of the people. This is very characteristic of the arrogance and contempt for the Russian people shown by many in Durnovo's class. Because of the lack of political consciousness, the argument goes, any revolution will be a socialist one. Once again he stresses the horrific consequences of war. Again he points to the distinction between the political classes and the popular class, where the former have no real support. On the whole this is in itself a shrewd judgement and the Bolsheviks, indeed, were very aware that they would have to provide the revolutionary leadership.

The final two sentences are again very contemptuous of the Russian people. The jibe about intellectuals (that is, those of liberal sentiments) appearing to the people as indistinguishable from government officials is very typical of the kind of reactionary stance Durnovo represents. There is, of course, much truth in what he says: Russia *was* a backward country and, what is almost worst, a leading member of the upper class expresses a kind of scoffing acceptance of this. But the last sentence may represent something of the kind of fatal miscalculation people like Durnovo were liable to make: not *all* workmen and peasants were so ignorant; some, particularly among the workers, were already showing political aspirations.

What is the document's significance in the study of total war and social change?

Even within this extract you can see that Durnovo is, in February 1914, envisaging war as a very real probability. With regard, then, to the question of the origins of World War I, this document is significant in showing that a senior politician fully expected war, which, in turn, serves to support the thesis that the question is not why war broke out in August 1914, but rather why it did not break out earlier. Within the extract, we can see that Durnovo is arguing that Russia should withdraw from an alliance which will involve it in war with Germany. So we can see that some conservatives in Russia, just as much as liberals in Britain, thought that an alliance between Britain and Russia was indeed unnatural. However, what the extract is mainly about is the perception that Russian society is so backward, and so divided, that war will inevitably lead to social revolution. The resigned pessimism of political figures like Durnovo was, of course, one of the things that was wrong with Russia, an attitude that made political reform so difficult. But the central significance is that we have here evidence of an experienced politician perceiving, *in advance*, the relationship between war and revolution.

Note that I have not here been providing a 'specimen answer'. Here I have been talking you through the *thought processes* involved in preparing yourself to write a commentary on an extract from a document.

1   THE NATURE OF TOTAL WAR

Introduction

Aggression may well be innate in human nature, but there is nothing 'natural' about war, let alone total war. Here, 'nature' is simply a term of art for the essential characteristics of the intensified, societal forms of warfare you have studied in AA312. The aim of this revision section is to look more closely at the concept of total war and to ask how and why the limited war that broke out in 1939 escalated into the most pervasive and unlimited conflict in history. What were the dynamics of this process of 'totalization'? Poles would rightly argue that, for their state and nation, the ordeal of total war began with the Nazi and Soviet invasions of 1 September and 17 September 1939. For Europe as a whole, however, there can be little argument that the globalization of the war, with the Nazi attack on the Soviet Union and the declaration of war on the United States, inaugurated collective violence on an unprecedented scale and led states to command huge proportions of their national economic resources in order to wage the conflict.

We find the changing nature of the war registered in the pronouncements of political leaders. In his broadcast to Germany of 4 September 1939, Neville Chamberlain declared: 'In this war we are not fighting against you, the German people, for whom we have no bitter feeling, but against a tyrannous and forsworn regime which has betrayed not only its own people but the whole of western civilization and all that you and we hold dear.' However conventional the utterance, it announced that Britain and her allies were engaged in a 'just war', and would conduct it humanely by discriminating between the enemy government and the German people. In practice, this distinction was impossible to maintain. In the autumn of 1940, Churchill could envisage no way of winning the war except by pressure of the blockade and the 'remorseless bombing of Germany and Italy'. Undermining enemy morale by area bombing became central to Allied strategy, which meant the indiscriminate killing of hundreds of thousands of civilians. Hitler did not cloak the attack on the Soviet Union with any spurious justification (as he had the declaration of war against Poland) and proclaimed it 'a war of annihilation' from the outset. His enemy responded in kind. When Stalin addressed CPSU and Red Army delegates in Moscow on 6 November 1941, on the eve of the anniversary of the Bolshevik Revolution, he declared: 'If they [the Germans] want a war of extermination, they shall have one.' For the western powers, total war was a process of escalation into which they were locked by the possibilities and constraints of the technology of destruction; on the eastern front, racist and totalitarian ideology determined that warfare was stripped of its vestigial moral limits from the outset.

I should like you now to read Hew Strachan, 'Total war in the twentieth century', reproduced as Chapter 15 in your Course Reader. This is a rather allusive essay, but worth persisting with because it makes an important distinction between 'modern war' and 'total war'. Whether or not you agree with Strachan's argument, you should find the essay thought-provoking. Please read it now.

The meanings of 'total war'

In Book 1, Unit 1, Arthur Marwick noted that you 'do not need to worry about the precise meaning of the term "total war": it is widely accepted in both academic and popular usage as being an effective description of the two major wars of the twentieth century' (p.9). Perhaps because the term is so widely accepted, nobody as far I know has bothered to define it. Should this concern us? I think it should because the phrase 'total war' can mean several things and, unless resolved, its ambiguities hinder historical analysis. One meaning is: war conducted to bring about the total defeat of the enemy – that is to say, achieving unconditional surrender overrides all political objectives. A second, closely related meaning is: warfare unlimited by any rules or conventions concerning the immunity of non-combatants, the treatment of prisoners and the rights of neutrals. By the 1930s, this meaning had become attached to the strategic doctrine that modern wars between great industrial powers had to be waged against whole populations. In Britain, it was thought of as a peculiarly German approach to war. During the Blitz, a government minister minuted to Churchill: 'In so far as the Germans may have been led by their theories of the total war into attacking our civilian population instead of concentrating upon our aircraft and air engine factories, it is very lucky for us' (Martin Gilbert, *Finest Hour*, 1983, p.878). A third meaning is: a conflict in which belligerent states call upon all available human and material resources to wage war, so that it ceases to be the sole concern of professional warriors and becomes the enterprise of whole societies.

These meanings are not logically exclusive, because wars have often involved disparate belligerents. We can cite instances of unlimited warfare conducted by small professional armies: after the Herero rebellion in German South West Africa (1904–7), the colonial authorities carried out a war of extermination against the native population. It was, writes H. U. Wehler, 'an early form of total war'. The military command proclaimed 'a war which did not allow for a peaceful solution' and which ended with the slaughter of half the Hereros and the deportation of a further quarter to prison camps, where there was a planned policy of genocide (Wehler, Introduction to *Imperialism*, 1979, p.132). Some wars between states have been grossly asymmetrical, with the result that one side committed a vastly greater proportion of its resources to the struggle than its opponents. Few societies have been more engaged in the common enterprise of war than Paraguay in its war with Brazil and Argentina between 1864 and 1870: four-fifths of Paraguayan men of military age were killed and the total population was halved.

There is a privileged use of the phrase 'total war' to refer to the world wars of the first half of the twentieth century. What it implies is that they were different from previous conflicts in their extent and destructiveness, in the scale of the forces involved and the degree of social mobilization required of the combatant states. The sheer loss of life would seem sufficient warrant for this privileged usage: total deaths attributable to World War I were between 10 and 13 millions; estimates of civilian and military deaths attributable to the Second World War vary between 45 and 50 millions. (A breakdown of Soviet and German war-related deaths is given below.) But if we infer from 'total' that these wars were wholly unprecedented or in some way aberrant conflicts in the course of

European history, then that is false. The conflicts of 1914–18 and 1939–45 were wars between coalitions of major military powers that pervaded and reshaped the international system of states. Such coalition wars had periodically raged across Europe since the Counter-Reformation, and spread far beyond its confines. As Jonathan Israel has remarked, the Dutch revolt against the Habsburgs could be claimed as the 'first global conflict in history': it was fought in the Americas, Africa and south-east Asia, as well as in Europe (Israel, *The Dutch Republic and the Hispanic World 1606–1661*, 1982, p.3). Furthermore, the mobilization of whole societies by the combatants during the twentieth-century total wars was an unintended outcome of two entwined processes in European political development: nation-state building and national identification on the part of the common people.

In this context, it is worth noting that even *before* the outbreak of the Second World War, Quincy Wright and his colleagues on the University of Chicago Causes of War Project were analysing the necessary and sufficient conditions for what he called the 'totalitarianization of war'. Wright argued that the *idea* of 'totalitarian war' could be traced to revolutionary and Napoleonic Wars, when the doctrine that the 'people' and the 'nation' are one legitimized mass mobilization such as the *ancien régime* had not attempted (Wright, *A Study of War*, 1942, vol.1, p.297). The precursors of the 'mobilized societies' of 1914–18 and 1939–45 were the major belligerents in the Napoleonic Wars. Military hardware in 1800 was much the same as in 1700, but the proportion of national resources spent waging war by the great powers had risen sharply. According to one estimate, central state expenditure in Britain in 1810 accounted for 37 per cent of national income (M. Mann, *The Sources of Social Power*, 1993, vol.2, Table 11.3). The accuracy of this figure is debatable, but there is no doubt that military spending, coupled with the financing of the anti-French coalition, imposed a public economic burden not matched until the First World War, when British government expenditure represented 52 per cent of national income. Clausewitz's concept of 'absolute war' (see Strachan, Course Reader, p.257) was, in a sense, a rationalization of the quantum leap in the scale of state belligerency in his own lifetime.[1]

Exercise   Strachan refers to 'a teleological view on the development and growth of modern war' (Course Reader, p.257) articulated by Raymond Aron and others in the aftermath of the Second World War. Could you summarize that view in a few sentences? ∎

Specimen answer   For Aron and his contemporaries, the advent of nuclear weapons – used to devastate Hiroshima and Nagasaki on 6 and 9 August 1945 – made Clausewitz's notion of 'absolute war' a reality. These weapons of mass destruction seemed the culmination of developments in strategic thinking and military technique that stretched back to Napoleon. Modern war had manifested an 'irrepressible dynamism' (Aron's phrase) which obliterated the distinction between combatants and civilians, spurred the belligerents into technological

[1] Carl von Clausewitz (1780–1831) served in the Prussian War School under Scharnhorst in the 1800s. He was seconded to the Tsarist Army in 1812, took part as a staff officer in the Battle of Borodino and saw at close quarters the retreat and disintegration of Napoleon's Grand Army.

competition in weaponry, and led to a relentless mobilization of national resources. The inherent tendency of modern war, so it seemed, was to subordinate ends to means and so become 'total'. □

Exercise   Does Strachan endorse the conflation of 'modern war' with 'total war'? If not, how does he distinguish between the two? Does making the distinction afford useful insights into the conduct of the Second World War? ∎

Specimen answer   No, Strachan does not endorse the conflation. He writes that 'A total war need not be modern, and a modern war need not be total' (Course Reader, p.263). For Strachan, what characterizes modern war is the exploitation of industrialism and science-based industry to produce the means of fighting. Modern war is *capital-intensive*, and states waging war with the most modern technology have tended to use manpower frugally. Total war is characterized both by indiscriminate violence against enemy populations and by belligerent states imposing 'absolute' demands on their own citizens. Because the two concepts are distinguishable, it is meaningful – and useful – to talk about 'de-modernization' during total war. A signal instance is the declining firepower of the German army on the eastern front after the battle of Kursk in June 1943, the largest engagement of armoured forces in history. Despite the fact that armaments output was rising rapidly, German industry was unable to keep pace with the eastern army's enormous losses of equipment, so the ratio of tanks, heavy weaponry and combat aircraft to fighting men went down. The *Wehrmacht* came to depend on its soldiers' moral qualities to endure an increasingly one-sided struggle. Japanese forces began the war with outdated equipment and the syndrome of 'de-modernization' was even more evident in the Pacific theatre.

Discussion   Total war is not uncommonly depicted as an outcome of 'modernity', and Strachan has done a valuable service in unpicking the relationship between the two. My reservation with his argument is that it rests on an uncomfortably narrow conception of the 'modern', which Strachan defines only in terms of industrialization and technological innovation. It is not easy to say what modernity was without being fatuously tautological, but all would agree that it had political as well as economic dimensions. However, whereas modern economies have adopted much the same technological infrastructure, modern states have taken manifestly different political forms: democratic and dictatorial, liberal and totalitarian. Though the Soviet economy was obviously more 'backward' than the American in the 1930s (income and productivity per head were far lower, a much greater proportion of the labour force remained in a primitive primary sector), the Soviet *state* had as good a claim to be 'modern' as the American. It had substituted planned economic development for the market irrationality that had made millions jobless throughout the capitalist world and was directing vast resources to improving the literacy, technical skills and the health status of the Soviet population. For many progressive intellectuals in Europe and elsewhere, this was 'the Enlightenment in power'.

Let me offer a perspective on modernization which tries to keep its political and economic aspects in view. No economy has ever existed outwith a political framework or state, and economic modernization has never occurred without major changes in the form of the state and the political relations between social classes. The structural change of industrialization – involving the reallocation of labour from agriculture to manufacturing and services – has invariably wrenched the political relations of agrarian polities out of joint. In the labour movement, urban workers created a form of social mobilization more threatening to autocratic and élite rule than peasant jacquerie because it nourished a popular demand for social democracy. There was, in other words, an endemic tension between the economic and political dimensions of modernity that, in terms of state structures, had a range of outcomes in late nineteenth- and early twentieth-century Europe. As Barrington Moore attempted to explain in a pioneer work of comparative historical sociology, 'states have taken different historical routes from the pre-industrial to the modern world' (Moore, *Social Origins of Dictatorship and Democracy*, 1966, p.xii). In some, the conflict between the popular demand for political equality and the market inequalities of a private enterprise economy resulted in the compromise of capitalist democracy. (Moore's examples were France, Britain, the US and India.) Other states (Russia, China) imploded in communist revolution. But in a third group (notably Germany, Italy and Japan) the tensions between economic and political modernization encouraged militaristic nationalism and right-wing authoritarianism. During the interwar world economic crisis, this route to political modernity culminated in fascism: a form of autarkic and racist nationalism whose leaders were prepared to resort to international war to achieve their territorial goals, just as they had waged internal war on domestic enemies.

Broadening our concept of modernity to include its political and ideological, as well its economic, dimensions, allows us to pursue Strachan's disaggregation of 'modern war' and 'total war' in a particularly useful way. The relationship between the Nazi dictatorship and modernity has long been a central issue in historical interpretations of the regime. The regime's ideology, and the source of its irrational destructiveness, was a utopian form of anti-modernism. The ideologically committed Nazis proposed 'to escape from the modern world by means of a desperate backward leap toward a romanticized vision of the harmony, simplicity and order of a world long lost' (H. A. Turner, 'Fascism and modernization', 1975, p.120). The demand for *Lebensraum* (living-space) was a crucial expression of this political atavism. The economic rationale for *Lebensraum* was the ending of Germany's dependence on imported foodstuffs and war materials. But it also had 'the socio-ethical purpose of opening the way to a vast new wave of German eastward colonization, making possible a significant degree of de-urbanization and de-industrialization' (ibid.). Millions of Germans were to be freed from factory labour because export goods would no longer be required to pay for imported foodstuffs. Hitler coupled his ideological anti-modernism with the irrational belief that war was 'the most powerful and classic expression of life' (*Hitlers Tischgespräche*, quoted in Ernst Nolte, *Three Faces of Fascism*, 1965, pp.409–10). A generation's peace, he maintained, spelt racial decadence for any nation. He anticipated a constant state of war in the east with equanimity, because it would strengthen the German race. Should the race prove 'unfit' for the epic struggle he had unleashed, he could contemplate its destruction with a bleak, Social Darwinian fatalism. When Barbarossa stalled before Moscow in late November 1941, Hitler told the Swedish foreign minister: 'If the German people are no longer so strong and ready for sacrifice that they will not stake their own blood on their existence, they deserve to pass away and be annihilated by another, stronger power' (quoted in J. C. Fest, *Hitler*, 1974, p.972).[2]

In practice, Nazi economic mobilization for a war of conquest subverted the regime's utopian goals. The labour requirements of rearmament accelerated the shift of workers from the land to industry: the proportion of the labour force employed in agriculture fell from 28.9 per cent in 1933 to 25.9 per cent in 1939; industry's share rose from 40.4 per cent to 42.2 per cent. The stepping up of munitions output from early 1942 brought an unprecedented boom in industrial investment: despite the bombing of much industrial plant, in 1945 the surviving capital stock (i.e. machinery and other producers' goods) in western Germany exceeded the pre-war level by one-fifth (W. Abelshauser, 'Germany: guns, butter, and economic miracles', 1998, p.146). On the eastern front, warfare may have been 'de-modernized'; on the home front, the foundations were being laid for the industrial resurgence of western Germany after the currency reform of June 1948 (A. S. Milward, *War, Economy and Society, 1939–1945*, 1977, p.78). German society was purged of its most conservative elements by military deaths, the destruction of the Prussian officer élite after the failed attempt on Hitler's life, and the territorial loss of East Prussia, Pomerania and Silesia. The consequences of launching a war of annihilation on the Soviet Union were to destroy the basis, within Germany, of the traditional resistance to modernity and liberalism, just as surely as Hitler had destroyed the structure of the *Rechtstaat* and democracy (G. A. Craig, *Germany 1866–1945*, 1981, p.764). □

From *Blitzkrieg* to total war

In discussing German strategy in the Second World War in Book 4, Unit 20, Clive Emsley alerts you to the contrast between *Blitzkrieg* (lightning war) and *totaler Krieg* (total war), but assumes that the meaning of the latter is self-evident. As you will recall, the path-breaking economic historians of Nazi Germany, B. Klein and A. S. Milward, identified *Blitzkrieg* as a strategic synthesis that allowed the National Socialist leadership to prepare for a series of short wars requiring no greater degree of commitment of the economy to war than already existed in 1938. The dictatorship feared a collapse of the home front if living standards were drastically curtailed by diverting resources from consumption to armaments. According to the long-accepted understanding of *Blitzkrieg*, the *Wehrmacht*'s failure to capture Moscow in the winter of 1941–42 marked the shift from a war involving limited economic mobilization to one in which military expenditure dominated economic activity. As you know, this interpretation has been challenged by R. J. Overy – who argues that the German economy was being mobilized for total war from 1936 – but it is broadly confirmed by the multi-authored study of the attack on the Soviet Union published by the *Militärgeschichtliches Forschungsamt* (Research Institute for Military History) (Boog *et al.*, *Germany and the Second World War*, vol.4, 1998). This massively researched volume devotes 1,250 pages to the preparations for Operation Barbarossa and military operations up to the turn of 1941–42. Even

---

[2] The English text misses out the 'not' before 'stake'; I have taken the liberty of inserting it.

experts must get lost in the forest of minutiae. But the gist of R. D. Müller's chapter on 'The failure of the economic "Blitzkrieg Strategy"' is quite clear. German war planners deliberately ran the war economy at far below its maximum capacity in 1940 and 1941. They believed that Barbarossa required only a limited armaments effort, which had already been largely completed in the spring of 1941. This was not a matter of military planning and economic planning getting out of synch. The leadership was so convinced of a quick victory that it relied totally on the success of military planning and neglected to mobilize those economic reserves which were still available for the war in the east. The economic planning undertaken by the various competing agencies was almost solely concerned with the exploitation of Soviet resources which, it was assumed, would quickly fall into German hands. No attempt was made to build up reserves of production before June 1941; almost all German war factories were still run on a one-shift basis until the end of the year. Nor did the planners address the known frictions within the war economy caused by sheer weakness of organization. Global industrial output did not rise significantly between 1939 and 1942 and the share of armaments in this total remained stuck at a relatively modest 16 per cent in 1940 and 1941 (see Table 28.1). The army's share of the armaments programme was reduced to boost the *Luftwaffe*'s and the navy's. The output of munitions was allowed to 'stagnate' (Müller's term) in the months before the attack (Müller, 'The failure of the economic "Blitzkrieg Strategy"', 1998, pp.1081–96).

Table 28.1 The net output of German industry, by industry group (1939–1944) (percentage of total)

	1939	1940	1941	1942	1943	1944
Armaments	9	16	16	22	31	40
Basic goods (iron and steel etc.)	21	22	25	25	24	21
Construction goods	23	15	13	9	6	6
Other investment goods	18	18	18	19	16	11
Consumer goods	29	29	28	25	23	22

(Source: Abelshauser, 1998, p.153)

The failure of the campaign plan and the unexpected extension of the German–Soviet war compelled the regime to co-ordinate its economic and armaments policy. Before the onset of winter, the firepower and mobility of the army's spearheads had been drastically reduced by the inability of German industry to compensate for the wastage of guns, tanks and motor vehicles (due as much to mechanical failure as to enemy action). The logistical difficulties of re-equipping divisions over huge distances exacerbated the problem of weapons supply but its root cause was exhausted stocks and the low level of new manufacture. By November, the problem was so acute that the chief of the army armaments programme thought it advisable to make peace as soon as possible. On the 29th, Fritz Todt, the Armaments Minister, advised Hitler to conclude a political peace. A tour of inspection by his Ministry's tank commission had revealed such deficiencies as to convince Todt the war could no longer be won (Müller, 1998, p.1180). When an exhausted Army Group Centre ground to a standstill before Moscow at the beginning of December 1941, Hitler finally ordered an increase in German armaments production. He had apparently recognized that the period of *Blitzkrieg* was over and that Germany faced a long war of attrition. Under the capable direction of Albert Speer, armaments production was brought under central control and reoriented in favour of the army. Civilian industrialists displaced the military as the dominant element in the armaments sector. Within two and a half years, global armaments output rose threefold, that of tanks increased sixfold. Military expenditure accounted for over three-quarters (76.5 per cent) of national income in 1943–44. To have devoted more resources to the military would have been self-defeating because certain civilian goods and services are vital for any society's functioning. As it was, Germany could make this level of economic commitment to the war only by mobilizing nearly eight million foreign workers. By September 1944, one-fifth of the labour force (and one in four in industry) were foreigners (many of them slave labourers). The German war effort was richly subsidized through the *Reich*'s occupation policies, which extracted 30–40 per cent of the wartime national products of France, the Netherlands and Norway. France provided Germany with as much food as and *more* industrial materials than all of the occupied USSR (M. Harrison, 'The economics of World War II: an overview', 1998, p.22). Fortunately, the Allies were able to make an even greater productive effort.

'Annihilating Jewish-Bolshevism': ideological total war

If Hitler did not intend to commit the German economy to total war in June 1941, he was nevertheless bent on the total destruction of the Soviet regime and prepared to wage war without restraint to achieve this end. On 3 March 1941, he instructed the High Command to revise its operational guidelines to conform with a war of annihilation:

> The impending campaign is more than a clash of arms; it also entails a struggle between two ideologies. To conclude this war it is not enough, given the vastness of the space, to defeat the enemy's forces. The entire territory must be dissolved into states with their own governments ... The Jewish-Bolshevik intelligentsia, as the oppressor of the past, must be liquidated.
>
> (Quoted in J. Förster, 'Operation Barbarossa as a war of conquest and annihilation', 1998, p.482)

A fortnight later, he told a conference of service chiefs:

> The intelligentsia put in by Stalin must be exterminated. The controlling machinery of the Russian empire must be smashed ... Force must be used in its most brutal form. The ideological ties holding together the Russian people are not yet strong and the nation would break up once the functionaries were eliminated.
>
> (Quoted in Förster, 1998, p.485)

The intention to wage unrestrained ideological war was embedded in two notorious decrees: the Führer decree of 13 May on the exercise of war jurisdiction in the Barbarossa area (which condoned in advance illegal measures taken by the *Wehrmacht* against enemy civilians) and the Order of 6 June to liquidate the Red Army's political commissars (Book 4, Unit 20, p.21). As German military lawyers acknowledged, both flouted international conventions on the conduct of war which the *Wehrmacht* had observed in the west in 1940. (Even in the Polish campaign, there had been no general High Command instructions in contravention of the laws of war, though the army had acted against guerrillas with the utmost rigour.) The ideological character of Barbarossa justified, in the eyes of political *and* military leaders, unremitting harshness. We must treat with dedicated scepticism General Halder's testimony to the Nuremberg War Crimes Tribunal (in Document II.1, *Primary Sources 2: Interwar and World War II*) that the generals were 'outraged' by the 'Commissar Order'. A draft of the Order was prepared within OKW (High Command of the Armed Forces) in May 1941, *on the initiative* of Lieutenant-General Müller and his legal adviser. It envisaged the 'liquidation' of all political functionaries, including Red Army commissars, captured by the army. Halder, who was then Chief of Army General Staff, commented on this draft: 'Troops must do their share in the ideological struggle of the eastern campaign' (quoted in Förster, 1998, p.508). And this they did. The army divisional reports for July–October 1941 routinely recorded the shooting of Soviet military commissars (easily recognized by their special badges) both in the field and in prisoner-of-war camps. The *Wehrmacht*'s complicity with the Nazis' ideological and racist aims was apparent from the day the border was crossed. The instructions to the troops issued by individual army commands echoed the conflation of 'Jew' and 'Bolshevik' that was fundamental to Nazi rhetoric. The occupying forces immediately removed from their public posts all Jews who had not fled, singled them out for forced labour, and ordered their registration and the wearing of distinguishing marks. By late July 1941, the evacuation of Jews and their confinement to ghettos was under way. Captured Red Army soldiers were urged to dispose of Jews and Bolshevik commissars in their midst.

The German military was equally complicit in a 'hunger strategy' directed against the Soviet population. Obtaining foodstuffs was one of the campaign's most important economic objectives. The Ministry of Food and OKW had jointly planned to gain control of Soviet food stocks so that the army could 'live off the land' and the maximum amount could be exported to the *Reich*. When this plan was discussed, it was clearly understood that implementing it would mean death by starvation for millions. In the event, the strategy had to be modified because there were too few occupying troops to get complete control of the harvest. Some concessions were made to the collective farm workers of the western Soviet Union to secure their co-operation. But supplies to the occupied towns were deliberately reduced to a trickle. Despite the protests of some occupation authorities, who needed to feed civilians working for the Germans and wanted to retain the goodwill of Ukrainians, in November maximum rations were decreed for townspeople which gave them virtually no chance of survival in the long term. (Jews, who constituted a large fraction of the urban population, were prescribed 420 calories a day.) By the middle of the month, the inhabitants of Kiev, the Ukrainian capital, were roaming the countryside to barter their furniture for food, while the peasants travelled to the city with farm wagons to fetch the goods they had been offered in return. Let it be said that ordinary

German soldiers, who were inclined to give some of their rations to needy civilians, had to be persuaded by their superiors to remain 'hard in the face of starving women and children'. (I quote OKW propaganda directed at German soldiers; quoted in Müller, 1998, p.1165.)

How many Soviet civilians died as a result of the 'hunger strategy' has not been precisely determined. Of the 17 million war-related deaths amongst the civil population, an estimated 11 million occurred in German-occupied territory. About 2.5 million were Russian Jews exterminated by the Nazis. Around 7 million deaths through malnutrition and hunger-related disease seems quite plausible. We can be sure, however, about the number of victims among the 3.35 million Soviet soldiers captured in 1941: by 1 February 1942, almost 60 per cent had died from starvation or hunger-related disease. (A further half million or so had been executed by the army and the SS.) Again, the German generals were at one with the political leadership in opposing humane treatment of Soviet prisoners of war. Some officials and industrialists urged that they be used to offset the severe labour shortage in the German economy, but this would have meant diverting foodstuffs from German civilians to feed the prisoners. About 700,000 Soviet captives were set to work, and they formed the last and weakest link in the German food chain. The unwillingness to impose austerity on the home front foreclosed more extensive use of captive labour. In anticipation of mass deaths in the prisoner-of-war camps, the military leadership launched 'an unrestrained propaganda of hate' in mid-October, in which they lambasted 'false' sympathy with the starving (Müller, 1998, p.1173). The Quartermaster General instructed unit commanders to reduce prisoners' rations drastically. They died because of a deliberate policy of extermination.

It needs emphasizing, however, that the barbarization of the eastern front was a two-sided process. The Soviet Union was not a signatory to the Geneva convention on prisoners of war and the Red Army treated German captives with merciless brutality from the very beginning, which encouraged a vicious circle of reprisals. On 29 June, the German 6th Army headquarters ordered that no prisoners were to be taken during its mopping-up operations in the rear in response to Red Army atrocities against captured German troops. In reporting the war for Soviet readers, journalists such as Ilya Ehrenburg openly incited the murder of German prisoners. That many were summarily executed is confirmed by captured sources emanating from the Soviet command agencies endeavouring to curb the practice, not on humanitarian grounds but because it encouraged German troops to resist to the bitter end (P. Hoffmann, 'The conduct of the war through Soviet eyes', 1998, p.915). Even if they were not summarily executed, German prisoners had slim chances of surviving: 90–95 per cent of those captured in 1941–42 perished. Moreover, Stalin's repressive state apparatus matched the Nazis' in wanton cruelty. When the *Wehrmacht* entered Soviet-occupied Poland, the Baltic states and the Ukraine, the NKVD massacred its prisoners. According to one estimate, 80,000–100,000 prisoners were shot in the Ukraine alone (Hoffmann, 1998, p.910). Hundreds were tortured to death rather than simply executed: in one prison, the floor was strewn with the tongues, eyes and ears of dead prisoners (R.J. Overy, *Russia's War*, 1998, p.82). The publicity given to these atrocities stifled any compunctions in the *Wehrmacht* about liquidating the Soviet regime's political representatives. We must add that the ideological stance of the Soviet state mirrored the aggressor's.

In his broadcast of 3 July, Stalin declared that this was no 'ordinary war' between opposing armies but a life and death struggle in which the Soviet people should 'have no pity for the enemy' who was to be ceaselessly pursued and annihilated. As we have already noted, Stalin echoed the Nazis in calling for 'a war of extermination' in November, and demanded 'No mercy for the German occupiers!' Since the Soviet regime was on the brink of destruction, there was an objective political necessity for this rhetoric. But it gave a warrant to meeting the enemy's savagery with savagery.

For the Germans, dreadful retribution for unleashing ideological total war came when the Soviet armies invaded the *Reich* in January 1945. Petty officials, such as local burgomasters, were shot out of hand. Families still occupying houses decked with Nazi insignia were slaughtered. The assault infantry astride their T34s mowed down columns of refugees. Soviet soldiers raped at will. Violated women were nailed by their hands to the farm-carts carrying their families (J. Erickson, *The Road to Berlin*, 1983, p.467). Although the front command finally intervened, with an order insisting on the restoration of military discipline and the implementation of the 'norms of conduct' towards the enemy population, rapes were condoned at the highest level. In conversation with Milovan Djilas, Stalin asked 'What is wrong with a Red Army soldier having his fun with a woman?'

Soviet mobilization for total war

It is unarguable that the eastern front was the epicentre of World War II in Europe. At least three-quarters of German battle casualties were in this theatre. Allowing for the losses amongst Germany's allies,[3] it probably claimed the lives of 12.5 million soldiers. The Soviet Union drafted over 30 million men; roughly two out of nine died (see Table 28.2). Germany was able to mobilize an even bigger proportion of its pre-war population, not least because foreigners were substituted for German working men. By the end of 1944, 30 per cent of Germany's working population had been called up: the highest military participation ratio of any state in World War II, and I would guess in modern history. Though absolute German losses were much lower than Soviet losses, proportionally they were higher: more than one in three German soldiers died. The western Allies were, by contrast, positively frugal with servicemen's lives. The British Commonwealth and the USA together lost only 940,000 men in all theatres of war; fewer than one in forty US servicemen died. To revert to Strachan's argument, they largely succeeded in fighting a 'modern' war. The Soviet–German conflict was 'total' in every sense of the word, and demanded an extraordinary degree of economic and social mobilization from both belligerents. But, for many reasons, Soviet society was placed under more intense stress for far longer. In understanding the nature of the war, it is essential to grasp the 'totality' of that social experience.

---

[3] Italy, Romania, Hungary and Slovakia together provided 100 divisions for the eastern front. There were also volunteer contingents from Spain, the Netherlands, Belgium and Vichy France.

Table 28.2   Soviet and German mobilization and losses in World War II

	Soviet		German	
	Millions	% of pre-war population	Millions	% of pre-war population
Military mobilization	30.6	16	13.0	19
Total losses	25.6	13	6.5	9
Military losses	8.7	4	4.5	6
Civilian losses	16.9	9	2.0	3

(Source: P. Gattrell and M. Harrison, 'The Russian and Soviet economies in two world wars: a comparative view', 1993, p.443)

Which of the belligerents in World War II mobilized the greatest proportion of its economic resources in order to wage total war? The answer, according to Table 28.3, was Germany, though military spending as a proportion of national income may have been greater in Japan in 1944. Whether this represented a greater economic 'effort' than the Soviet Union's is debatable. The USSR was a poorer, less developed economy, with a smaller surplus of resources over basic subsistence. Per capita income in 1940 was about two-fifths the German level; 57 per cent of the Soviet labour force still worked in agriculture, where output per worker was only one-third of Soviet industry. Machinery was relatively much more expensive in the capital-poor Soviet economy than in Germany, Britain or the US, so it was far more costly to mechanize Soviet fighting forces. Added to which, the Soviet economic experience was very different from the German and the British (and the complete opposite of the American). In Germany, gross domestic product (GDP) grew quite significantly between 1939 and 1944, though the rate of growth was greater in Britain, where there had still been 1.25 million unemployed at the outbreak of war. (In the US, GDP and real per capita income soared from 1941. Millions entered the labour force who would not otherwise have been employed.) The Soviet Union's national product *fell* by more than a third in 1941–42 and remained significantly below the pre-war level in 1945. Despite some strategically motivated industrial relocation in the 1930s, heavy industry was still concentrated in the southern and western regions of European USSR when the Germans attacked. Between July and November 1941, the Soviet authorities managed to evacuate about one-eighth of all industrial

Table 28.3   Military outlays as a percentage of national income

	1942	1943	1944
Germany	64	70	75*
Japan	33	43	76
UK	52	55	53
USA	31	42	42
USSR	61	61	53

* approximate figure
(Source: Harrison, 'The economics of World War II: an overview', 1998, p.21)

assets, but a great swathe of vital economic resources was either destroyed or fell into enemy hands. Because of territorial losses, the Soviet Union fought the war's decisive battles with a capital stock no more than two-thirds the size of that already accumulated in 1940.

The comparative backwardness of the Soviet economy, and the huge material losses of 1941–42, compelled the state to take the most extreme measures to mobilize *human* resources. All data on labour mobilization show that no other belligerent diverted so much of its population to work for the war effort, and none demanded such heavy and prolonged sacrifices from its people. In February 1942 all able-bodied men aged between 16 and 55 and all women aged between 16 and 45 (later raised to 50) who were not already employed in state enterprises or establishments were mobilized for work in industry or construction. Avoiding the labour draft was made a criminal offence. In the spring, measures were taken to mobilize the urban population for agricultural labour. In September, employees of state enterprises located close to the front who left their jobs without permission were deemed 'deserters', to be tried by military tribunal. The railway workforce was subsequently placed under martial law. Absenteeism from work was severely prosecuted wherever it occurred: there were about one million convictions per war year.

Other states (most notably Britain) took similar steps to mobilize labour, but theirs were not so far-reaching nor so draconically enforced. Women's employment affords a good, comparative index of the degree of societal commitment to waging war. It is true that the greatest proportional increases in women's wartime employment took place in Britain: 80 per cent of the total addition to the labour force between 1939 and 1943 consisted of women who had not previously been employed or had been housewives (Milward, *War, Economy and Society, 1939–1945*, 1977, p.219). But the big influx of women into paid work was partly a reflection of their relatively low rate of labour force participation in 1939. In the Soviet Union, where a larger proportion of women were already employed in peacetime, they became a clear majority of industrial workers and an overwhelming majority of farm workers in what was still a predominantly agricultural economy. German agriculture also became a women's preserve (females formed nearly two-thirds of the farm labour force by 1945) but German industry drew much less on women's work than did the

Table 28.4   Females as a percentage of the civilian labour force in Britain, the Soviet Union and Germany

	1939	*1940*	*1941*	*1942*	*1943*	*1944*	*1945*
Britain	27	30	33	37	39	39	38
Germany	37	40	39	40	40	41	42
USSR: public sector	–	38	–	53	57	57	55
USSR: collective farming	–	–	52	62	73	78	80

(Sources: HMSO, *Statistical Digest of the War*, 1951; V. R. Berghahn, *Modern Germany*, 1987, Table 32; J. Barber and M. Harrison, *The Soviet Home Front 1941–1945*, 1991, Table 4)

Soviet Union (35 per cent of industrial workers were women in Germany in 1944, compared with 53 per cent in the Soviet Union).

Soviet employment statistics demonstrate a colossal 'reshaping' of the labour force between 1940 and 1942, when the total working population fell by over 30 million (chiefly because of the German occupation). The government had to compensate for huge losses in civilian labour and military personnel while expanding the armed forces two and half times and redirecting industrial workers to munitions output. As you will see from Table 28.5, agriculture was its principal source of manpower: while the total working population fell by 37 per cent, the farm workforce declined by 52 per cent. (Farm tractors and horses were also requisitioned, which had a calamitous impact on the productivity of the remaining workforce.) Three out of five Red Army recruits came from the countryside. But every branch of 'non-essential' employment was stripped of labour for the armed services and the war economy. During 1942, over 47 per cent of the working population was either in the forces or employed in the supply of goods and services paid for out of the defence budget.

Paradoxically, the proportion of the Soviet labour force directly producing armaments was the lowest of the major combatants because a large, unproductive agricultural sector inescapably constrained industrial mobilization. You will see from Table 28.5 that industry's share of total employment in 1942 and 1943 was just under 16 per cent. About half of all industrial workers (or 8 per cent of total employment) worked in munitions, engineering, shipbuilding, metalworking and chemicals. The comparable figure in Germany and the US was 15 per cent. In Britain, the world's most highly industrialized economy, it was 24 per cent. But Britain's agriculture was highly efficient, and imports still provided most food requirements; its industrial structure and seapower meant a relatively smooth adaptation to a long war of production. The Soviet economy, by contrast, was desperately *over*-mobilized until mid-1943, and in danger of collapsing into chaos. The numbers employed producing civilian goods and services fell from roughly 72 million in 1940 to perhaps 28 million in 1942. 'This was a shock of unprecedented scale' (Barber and Harrison, *The Soviet Home Front 1941–1945*, 1991, p.147). Basic consumer goods – clothing and food – were in desperately short supply. Consumer services atrophied while demand for such services soared: there were 25 million homeless people to be fed and housed. Civilian life was reduced to a miserable shambles that posed a deadly threat to the continuity of defence production.

Many were debilitated by chronic hunger if not actually starving to death. In 1942–43, agricultural output was a mere third of that of 1940. Per head of population, the total food available in 1943 from Soviet sources was only 56 per cent of the pre-war amount. Controlling the food supply was not just a matter of balancing fairness and efficiency, but of famine management. A rationing system ensured that the armed forces and munitions workers had sufficient food (though over four-fifths of their nutrition came from bread) and differentiated rations were used to attract labour to the most arduous occupations. But most people's rations fell well short of minimum nutritional levels. White-collar workers and dependants, particularly children over the age of 12, were especially discriminated against. Poor diet reduced women's fertility, and so contributed to the steep fall in the birth-rate (Barber and Harrison, 1991, p.82). Furthermore, the ration system excluded about half the population. Collective farm workers, for example, had no ration entitlement, though official procurements of cereals and meat were significantly intensified. Rural folk relied on their private plots. A tiny number of farmers became rouble millionaires from selling foodstuffs at greatly inflated prices on the tolerated free markets; the vast majority endured very hard times. The number of Gulag prisoners starving to death rose steeply. A large proportion of the 3 million wartime deportees (mostly ethnic Germans and Chechens) suffered the same fate.

Table 28.5   Soviet employment in wartime (millions)

	1940	1941	1942	1943	1944	1945
Armed forces	4.2	7.5	10.9	11.1	11.2	11.6
Industry	13.1	11.9	8.3	8.6	9.4	11.2
Transport, trade, construction	9.5	10.3	5.9	6.2	8.5	–
Agriculture	49.7	36.9	24.0	25.1	30.6	–
Civilian services	8.6	6.1	4.3	4.7	5.6	
Total working population	85.1	72.8	53.3	55.6	65.3	74.6

(Source: Barber and Harrison, 1991, Table 9)

Unlike their Tsarist predecessors, Soviet administrators managed both to impose order on economic chaos and to organize munitions supply at roughly twice the rate of German industry and well in excess of the British rate. This was a signal contribution to the Allies' advantage over the Axis powers in military resources, and one quite disproportionate to the size and development of the Soviet industrial economy. The clear superiority of Soviet tank and aircraft production is evident in Table 28.6; figures for heavy guns and shells tell a similar story. This superiority – achieved by a dramatic rise in output per worker in munitions – was an essential precondition for military recovery. The 'wastage' of Red Army equipment in the first year of the war was quite staggering: front-line forces lost one-sixth of their aircraft, one-seventh of their guns and mortars and one-tenth of their armoured equipment *every week* in the winter of 1941–42. For every German tank destroyed, the Red Army lost seven. Soviet industry had to make good these losses and enable the Red Army to accumulate superior resources to those of the *Wehrmacht*. Soviet soldiers had matchless tenacity but were generally inferior to the Germans in tactics, combat organization and the handling of modern weaponry. Their numerical superiority was not as great as you might infer from Table 28.2: in late 1944, there were 12.2 million men in the Soviet forces, and 12.4 million in the German. The Red Army was victorious because it acquired overwhelming firepower, which it learnt to use with greater economy than in 1941–42. A typical infantry division's firepower quadrupled over the war years. New armies were built round the tank corps: a fast-moving unit armed with 168 tanks, anti-tank battalions, Katyusha rockets and anti-aircraft artillery. Two tank corps combined with an infantry division made up a tank army: a self-contained and highly mobile fighting instrument. By the autumn of 1944 the ratio of Soviet to German tank losses was down to one to one.

In the defensive battles that broke the back of the German army in 1942–43, the Red Army's superiority in *matériel* was attributable almost entirely to Soviet industry. In the gigantic offensives that drove the Germans out of the Soviet Union, the Red Army was much indebted to lend-lease shipments for its mobility and battlefield communications. Western aid deliveries (in the form of military equipment, food and industrial raw materials) amounted to roughly 15 per cent of Soviet defence spending in 1943–44. Seventeen per cent of the combat aircraft, 12 per cent of armoured fighting vehicles, and most military radios and field telephones used by Soviet forces over the course of the war were supplied by the western Allies. (In effect, the Americans. Britain shipped some *matériel* to the Soviet Union, but British forces depended much more on lend-lease equipment than did Soviet forces. Any surplus military stocks in Britain were the result of American aid.) This was probably not a 'war-winning' margin but it contributed significantly to the speed of the Soviet advance in 1944–45 and so to shortening the war.

Table 28.6   Production of armour and combat aircraft by the major powers in 1941–45 (in 000s)

	Tanks and self-propelled guns	*Combat aircraft*
USSR	102.8	112.1
Germany	43.4	79.6
Britain	27.6	84.7
USA	99.5	192.0

(Source: Harrison, 'The economics of World War II: an overview', 1998, Table 1.6)

The 'totalization' of war by the western Allies: the strategic bombing of Germany

The western Allies' chosen instrument for waging total war against Germany was strategic bombing. By this we mean the use of long-range bombers against civilian targets in the hope of destroying economic resources and undermining morale. What, essentially, distinguishes strategic bombing from the tactical use of airpower in support of ground forces is that it assigns bombers an *autonomous* role in grand strategy. Before 1939, the unrestricted bombing of civilian targets had been seen as part and parcel of a 'totalitarian' era: Italian Fascists bombed defenceless Ethiopian villagers with poison-gas shells; the Nazi Condor Legion bombed Guernica on behalf of the Spanish Nationalists. In the event, the civilian-led democracies far outdid the dictatorships in the systematic bombing of civilians. British night-time bombing originated in the autumn of 1940 but for over two years met with scant success: the bombers were 'light' machines, not yet equipped with electronic aids for night navigation, that usually missed their targets. We can date the commitment of really significant Allied resources to strategic bombing to Churchill's meeting with Stalin in

October 1942, when the Prime Minister was goaded by accusations of cowardice into revealing plans for the heavy bombing of Germany, and to the Casablanca conference of the western Allies of January 1943 (Unit 20, p.18). It was then that Churchill and Roosevelt agreed to intensify the air campaign with the 'heaviest possible bomber offensive against the German war effort'. Neither expected bombing alone to bring about the defeat of Germany, but both assigned it a far greater role in waging total war than did either Hitler or Stalin. The western leaders were, it is important to note, acting against the advice of most of their military advisers. By this stage of the war, military professionals everywhere were disillusioned with the extravagant claims made for the potency of bombing in the 1930s. Churchill, who had once been an enthusiast, penned an incisive critique of bombing in September 1941.

> It is [he wrote] very disputable whether bombing by itself will be a decisive factor in the present war ... all that we have learnt since the war began shows that its effects, both physical and moral, are greatly exaggerated ... it seems very likely that the [German] ground defences and night fighters will overtake the Air attack ... [I]n calculating the number of bombers necessary to achieve hypothetical and indefinite tasks, it should be noted that only a quarter of our bombs hit the targets.
>
> (Quoted in Gilbert, *Finest Hour*, 1983, p.1205)

In May 1942, an enquiry into the operational effectiveness of bombing showed that the premier's estimate of its accuracy was decidedly optimistic: fewer than a quarter of the bombs dropped fell within five miles of the designated target, and only 30 per cent hit built-up areas. Right up to the Casablanca conference, there were mounting arguments against bombing's cost-effectiveness and for the diversion of material and human resources from Bomber Command's campaign to more worthwhile undertakings.

Exercise   Why, despite its hitherto paltry results and the opposition of their military advisers, did western leaders commit themselves to intensifying the bombing campaign? ■

Specimen answer   As you will probably have gathered, political considerations largely determined their decision. Allied service chiefs had concluded that they would be unable to open a 'second front' before the spring of 1944. Bombing was the only means of placating Stalin: it demonstrated that Britain and America were in earnest about killing Germans. I would give just as much weight to another political consideration: Churchill and Roosevelt were responsible leaders of democracies. Stalin's regime could treat its own soldiers according to what one retired Soviet general called 'the inhuman slogan' that 'human lives must not be spared' (Major-General Grigorenko, quoted in Hoffmann, 'The conduct of the war through Soviet eyes', 1998, p.909). This option was not open to Churchill and Roosevelt: to retain public support for the Allied war effort, they had to minimalize casualties in their own forces. Bombing promised to do that. □

A further point worth emphasizing (though not mentioned in Unit 20) is that when the US entered the war in December 1941, it had already committed vast resources to manufacturing heavy bombers. In May, Roosevelt ordered the production of 500 a month (Britain produced just 498 in the whole of 1941)

(Overy, *Why the Allies Won*, 1995, p.109). Heavily armed US bombers, operating in daylight, were supposed to be able to do what Bomber Command flying by night could not: hit precise, industrial targets. The huge investment already made in this arm of warfare was a compelling reason to use it.

The British had also invested considerable technological effort in improving their performance. At the end of 1942, the four-engined Lancaster bomber – which could carry heavier loads a greater distance than its twin-engined predecessors – came into service, and radio navigational devices were developed that allowed for greater concentrations of destructive force. Though they did not make night bombing much more precise, they did make 'area' bombing more effective. German fire and other emergency services could deal with the effects of bombing dispersed over time and space, but saturation bombing started self-sustaining fires, disrupted water supplies and made roads impassable. When this concatenation of blows fell on a city's infrastructure, area bombing could achieve its intended effect of 'de-housing' much of the population and bringing industrial activity to a halt. In late July–August 1943, one million residents of Hamburg were driven to seek refuge outside the urban area after incendiary bombing had created a fire-storm. Two-thirds as many people were killed as died in all the German raids on Britain. As it happened, this feat was difficult to repeat in Europe because of factors outside Allied control: the Hamburg raids were preceded by a prolonged spell of hot weather which left the city's many timber-framed buildings tinder dry. Japanese cities presented similarly vulnerable targets in the spring and summer of 1945: about 120,000 of Tokyo's inhabitants were killed or injured in a devastating fire-storm on 9 March. But the only other German city destroyed by fire-storm was Dresden, which was incinerated by successive night and day raids in February. The city was swollen with refugees fleeing from the east, so civilian deaths were appallingly high, although the destruction was so terrible that they could not be reliably estimated. Rightly, photographs of Dresden have become thickly textured with meaning – we see not just ruins but gratuitous destruction and the degradation of the Allied cause – and have entered that repertoire of cultural images which represents for us the 'totality' of twentieth-century war. It was not, alas, the end of the bombing offensive: in March 1945, German targets received a weight of bombs almost equal to that dropped by Bomber Command during the whole of 1943.

Two questions have dominated the debate over the strategic bombing campaign virtually since the cessation of hostilities: was it morally right, and was it militarily worthwhile? The first question continues a long-standing argument in western moral philosophy and jurisprudence over the proper conduct of a 'just war'. (Michael Walzer, *Just and Unjust Wars*, 1980, remains the best introduction to this topic.) Although historical research cannot settle this argument, it can contribute something to it by tracing the steps by which democratic leaders and their military advisers overcame their own moral scruples about the indiscriminate bombing of civilians. If their arguments for the end justifying the means in this context were well-articulated and cogent, then that must carry a certain weight in the moral arguments of subsequent generations. The second question is more properly historical. Those who criticized bombing on the grounds of its poor cost-effectiveness found a seemingly unimpeachable source in the survey conducted by US officials in 1945, *The Effects of Strategic Bombing on the German War Economy.* This concluded that the inaccuracy of bombing and the great expense of mounting the campaign (in terms of capital costs and the lives of highly trained aircrews) made it an inefficient way of waging war. Bombing had not stopped the German industrial economy from growing: in May 1945, there were substantially more machines, and more productive capacity, amidst the rubble of urban Germany than there had been in September 1939. It was calculated that, in 1943, bombing reduced Germany's total production by only about 9 per cent, and in 1944 by 17 per cent; and less than half of this reduction was in armaments. Moreover, bombing, like any other undertaking, had what economists call 'opportunity costs': the capital, labour and human ingenuity invested in bombers and aircrew could not go into tanks, artillery and mechanized infantry or anti-submarine warfare. Both, according to the survey, would have represented a better return on investment. Many historians have concurred. David French, for example, writes: 'The strategic bombing offensive cost the lives of 100,000 British, Commonwealth and American aircrew and perhaps between three-quarters of a million and one million Germans. It was a major misapplication of resources' (quoted in A.W. Purdue, *The Second World War*, 1999, p.142).

A robust defence of the effectiveness of the bombing offensive has been mounted by Overy in his admirable analytic history of the war. As he emphasizes, bombing compelled the Germans to divert their airpower from the battle fronts in order to protect the *Reich*. For much of its duration, the bombing offensive was a fighting contest between the Allied air forces and the *Luftwaffe*. This contest was transformed by the simple expedient of fitting extra fuel tanks to Allied fighters, so enabling them to escort bomber 'streams' deep into Germany. The 'mighty' P51 Mustang, which came into service in late 1943, proved exceptionally capable, and was soon being produced in enormous quantities in American factories. By the spring of 1944, half the *Luftwaffe*'s fighters and a quarter of its pilots were being lost each month in hopelessly unequal combat with Mustangs, Lightnings and Thunderbolts. The eastern front was denuded of German aircraft: by April there were only 500 single-engine fighters facing over 13,000 Soviet aircraft (Overy, *Why the Allies Won*, 1995, p.142). With the *Luftwaffe* virtually destroyed, the Allies threw massive firepower against Germany's industrial fabric and transport infrastructure. Because freight movement was drastically reduced, the economy was fragmented into isolated regions by the end of 1944. On 30 January 1945, Speer sent Hitler a memorandum informing him that 'The war is over in the area of heavy industry and armaments ... from now on the material preponderance of the enemy can no longer be compensated for by the bravery of our soldiers' (quoted in Overy, 1995, p.125).

And what of the failure of bombing to curb the growth of German armaments production between 1941 and 1944? Undoubtedly, the economic effects of bombing were much exaggerated in 1942–43, but the proper question to ask is what Germany could have produced had the bombing not become so intense. With much of continental Europe at its disposal, the Nazi regime commanded enormous economic resources. Bombing placed a strict ceiling on the expansion of munitions production: according to Speer, the planned output of tanks, aircraft and military vehicles in 1944 was reduced by around 35 per cent as a result of bombing (Overy, 1995, p.131). So did US officials err in their modest estimate of the impact of bombing on the German war economy? Their calculations involved more guesswork than is commonly appreciated and some of the academic economists and statisticians temporarily in government service had a deep moral distaste for this method of waging war. They saw the stocks of undamaged machinery, marvelled at the resilience of the civilian population, and almost certainly underestimated the tremendous dislocation of the German war effort.

Conclusions

It is clear that the western Allies and the Soviet Union waged very different kinds of wars: the former equipped themselves for capital-intensive warfare and conserved their manpower; the latter expended huge drafts of military labour. Germany's experience lay somewhere between the two. Superior combat organization almost brought military victory over the numerically larger Red Army in 1941–42; had the Soviet Union been knocked out of the war, the Third *Reich* would have been unassailable. As it was, Hitler succeeded in creating an opposing coalition that commanded overwhelming industrial resources. Germany was forced into fighting a war that was both capital and labour intensive. These states were all engaged in the same conflict; were they all waging total war? This is not just a trivially semantic question because it requires us to think about the demands states placed on their own populations *as well as* the methods employed to destroy the enemy. Probably an equal number of German civilians died as a result of the western Allies' bombing offensive as were killed by the advancing Red Army; both waged unrestricted, inhumane war. Taking the war to German civilians was a more considered and rationalized part of the western Allies' strategy. But with respect to the mobilization of their own populations, the western and Soviet governments behaved in fundamentally different ways. In the democracies, something like a bargain was struck between the state and the people. Wartime governments entered new social contracts with organized labour. Although the state subjected workers to more exacting demands and curtailed the right to strike, it facilitated trade union organization and extended the socio-economic rights of citizenship. No such bargain was struck in the Soviet Union: in material terms, the state had little to bargain with. It could only divide diminishing total resources so as to maximize output. Those least useful to the national war effort, such as the elderly, were condemned to terrible privation. Soviet workers were not just motivated by patriotism and hatred of the invader, though these were powerful emotions. They were also coerced by a vast repressive state apparatus. The ration card was a marvellous instrument of social discipline; the most indisciplined and truculent could be threatened with deportation and imprisonment. The forced-labour camps made a formidable contribution to the Soviet war effort: they produced approximately 15 per cent of all Soviet ammunition, including 9.2 million anti-personnel mines and 25.5 million large-calibre shells. Over two million prisoners were used on railways and roads, in mines and lumber plants. Notwithstanding some liberalization in religious life, in the balance of the Soviet war effort coercion played a bigger role than consensus and had a more lasting impact on social life. The late Stalinist state of 1945–53 is a glaring counter-example to theories of total war and social change that posit the flattening of the pyramid of social inequality through the participation of the underprivileged in the war effort. In these theories, 'total war' is a black box rather than an explanatory concept. We need to pick it apart to see precisely what was entailed in fighting the enemy and mobilizing resources.

2   THE CAUSES OF WAR

As part of this course you have studied the origins of the First and Second World Wars, and it is quite likely that you will be asked in the exam to analyse their causes. This section will go over some of the arguments advanced in previous units, and review some of the issues that have formed a sub-theme of the course.

Exercise

It is important to distinguish between *immediate* causes, which occasioned or triggered the outbreak of wars, and their longer-term or underlying causes. Thinking back to Units 5 and 19, what would you say were the immediate causes of war in August 1914 and September 1939? ■

Specimen answer and discussion

Identifying the immediate causes of the First World War in July–August 1914 is not altogether a simple matter. The assassination of Archduke Franz Ferdinand on 28 June 1914 was the spark which ignited a general European war. But was the assassination simply seized on by Austria-Hungary as a pretext for its intention to deal 'once and for all' with Serbia, and should we therefore identify the immediate cause in the Austrian ultimatum to Belgrade on 23 July? Berlin's 'blank cheque' to Vienna might also count as an immediate and perhaps a more significant cause of the war: it enabled Austria-Hungary to adopt a tough stance vis-à-vis Serbia with the assurance of Germany's unconditional backing, thereby risking the widening of the conflict. As we have seen, the primary evidence assembled by Fritz Fischer, Imanuel Geiss and others shows conclusively that the German government bore a large share of responsibility for escalating the crisis and deliberately risking a European war. However, other European nations also took fateful decisions in July 1914. Russia's determination to support Serbia, and Britain's reluctance to make a firm and clear statement of intent until it was too late for German and Austrian statesmen to reverse their course of action, may both be regarded as immediate causes of the war.

The immediate cause of war in 1939 does not appear to present the same problems: the German attack on Poland (31 August) was for Britain and France, both guarantors of Polish independence, the *casus belli* (the event giving rise to and justifying the war). It is worth emphasizing, however, that it was they who took the decision to turn a limited war into a *general* war by issuing ultimata to Germany. In explaining the outbreak of the Second World War we have, therefore, to accord as much attention to the calculations and miscalculations of the British and French governments as we do to those of Hitler. □

Exercise

What was common to the expectations of the men responsible for the outbreak of war in 1914? ■

Specimen answer and discussion

The war that ensued in 1914 was quite different from the one expected by the men responsible for its outbreak. In August 1914 nearly everyone thought that the fighting would be over within six months, if not by Christmas, and this 'short-war illusion' must be considered part of the atmosphere (or of the 'unspoken assumptions', in James Joll's phrase) that aided the advent of war. The men of 1914 were not exceptional in deluding themselves, for similar misjudgements had been made before the start of many previous wars, although the experience of recent wars (such as the American Civil War, the Boer War and the Russo-Japanese War) should have suggested to them that the coming war would differ from nineteenth-century cabinet wars. Indeed, recent research into the attitudes of the German General Staff has revealed an awareness of the

Hindenburg

possibility of a future war being a long war of attrition. This was an accurate prediction, but not one which the military leaders chose to share with the responsible politicians, who continued to believe, like the people whose fates they controlled, that the coming war would be over quickly (Stig Förster, 'Der deutsche Generalstab und die Illusion des kurzen Krieges, 1871–1914: Metakritik eines Mythos', 1995). □

Exercise   Did those responsible for its outbreak expect a world war in August 1939? ∎

Specimen answer and discussion   In late August 1939, Hitler was convinced that the result of his non-aggression pact with Russia of 23 August would be to localize his conflict with Poland and turn the tables on Britain and France, who, he felt certain, would back down and stay out. Chamberlain for his part had believed a pact between such sworn ideological enemies as Nazi Germany and Communist Russia to be inconceivable. When it happened, he had either to stand by his word to Poland, or see his bluff called and himself out of office. To the last he hoped for a peaceful solution on the Munich model. He was pushed into declaring war by parliamentary pressure. 'On any rational calculation', as A. J. P. Taylor says, 'the Nazi-Soviet pact ought to have discouraged the British people' (*The Origins of the Second World War*, 1964, p.323). It did not. Taylor is thus right to point out that the immediate outbreak of war in 1939 was 'the result on both sides of diplomatic blunders' (p.269). On both occasions, then, in 1939 as in 1914, false expectations contributed to the outbreak of conflict, and on neither occasion did those responsible for the outbreak of war envisage or want a war of the scale and duration that it turned out to be. □

So far in our discussion of the origins of the two world wars, we have concentrated on the immediate causes. If they are difficult to establish, the longer-term causes are even harder to ascertain.

Exercise   Try to think of some long-term causes of the First and Second World Wars. ∎

Specimen answer   For the First World War, you might have mentioned the alliance system, international rivalries, the arms and naval race, imperialism, German *Weltpolitik*, Pan-Slavism, nationalist tensions in the Balkans and so on. We cannot discuss them all here, but it will help with your exam preparation if you reread Unit 5, which deals with some of these long-term causes at length.

For the Second World War, you might – again – have mentioned international alliances. You might have advanced the argument that the roots of the Second World War were, if not in the First World War itself, then at least in the Versailles peace settlement (a view that will be further discussed below), and that Germany's desire for revenge and for a more prominent position at the heart of Europe was one of the reasons why war broke out in 1939. □

Exercise   What arguments can you advance in support of the view that the two world wars had a common cause in imbalances (both actual and potential) within the great power system? ∎

Specimen answer and discussion   One might preface an answer by saying that the multipolar world of 1914 and 1939 was inherently more unstable than the bipolar world created by the Second World War and the nuclear stalemate. On the eve of the First World War, eight powers (France, Britain, Germany, Austria-Hungary, Russia, Italy, the US and Japan) had the capacity to sustain industrialized warfare against each other. Although they were highly unequal in their resources, the disparity between them was not such as to create a super-power hegemony and each was free to pursue aggressive adventures abroad. (Japan attacked China and Russia, Italy fought Turkey over Libya, and the US went to war with Spain.)

That said, a more threatening source of international instability lay in an historically novel type of imbalance that had arisen between the established imperial and continental powers, and the rising power of Germany. Britain and France were global states by virtue of their Asian and African empires; for both, pacifying and conserving imperial possessions was a major aim of national policy which (despite the 1898 war scare known as the Fashoda crisis – see Roberts, p.96, for details) they were able to pursue without disturbing the international balance. The US and Russia were steadily expanding into their vast land masses and – whatever their military and political weaknesses – their status as great powers was assured by their territorial, demographic and material resources. □

Germany's ruling class felt that their country's position within the great power system was anomalous: it was undoubtedly Europe's leading industrial and military state, but (it was thought) it did not exercise a global power commensurate with its economic strength, demographic vitality and military traditions. Whether these perceptions were 'objectively' valid is beside the point, for from 1897 they led Germany to embark upon *Weltpolitik*, a conscious and determined quest for 'world power' status, and to challenge British naval supremacy by building a High Sea Fleet. Germany's decision-makers justified this threat to British naval hegemony by conjuring up fears of 'encirclement', but the naval arms race actually turned the fears it was meant to dispel into reality. Britain felt forced to end its 'splendid isolation', first by concluding an alliance with Japan in 1902, and then (more importantly from Germany's point of view) by forming an entente in 1904 with France, which had been allied to its former enemy Russia since 1894. In 1906, the British and French General Staffs began secret talks about a co-ordination of the military strategy, and in 1912 Britain undertook naval commitments to France so binding that it is highly likely it would have been drawn into a Franco-German war even if Germany had not violated Belgian neutrality.

Restoration of the equilibrium which had been disturbed by Germany's 'world power' policy was, for Britain, the motive for the entente with France and Russia. Many would argue, too, that the British decision for war both in 1914 and in 1939 was determined by the conviction that a German victory would destroy the existing balance and create a new one totally inimical to British interests. Following a policy traditional since the sixteenth century, it was seen as in Britain's vital interests to oppose the dominant continental power of the time: Habsburg Spain, the France of Louis XIV and Napoleon, and Wilhelmine Germany. In 1914 and in 1939, Britain took the view that if Germany conquered the Low Countries or France, then Britain's independence would be directly threatened by a German hegemony on the continent. In both cases, if Britain did not stand by France, its credibility as an ally would be at stake. On both occasions there was speculation that France, if abandoned by Britain, would make terms with Germany, leaving Britain isolated and at Germany's mercy. In this sense, the invasion of Belgium and of Poland in 1914 and 1939 respectively was the occasion for, rather than the cause of, British intervention. The cause was the preservation of the balance of power. Moreover, in 1914 that balance was further threatened by Russia's expanding power in the east, and the potential threat it posed to India. As we have seen, some historians would argue that Britain went to war in 1914 because a victorious Russia might have become a potent future enemy for the British Empire, and it was thought that only by being Russia's ally could such future enmity be averted. The balance-of-power concept does, therefore, help us understand both the alignment of international forces in the twentieth century and Britain's participation in the war (which both in 1914 and in 1939 was contrary to Germany's expectations).

This exposition has referred to the *perceptions* of Germany's political class, the *motives* behind British foreign policy, and – by implication – how decision-makers in both states *interpreted* the concept of the balance of power. The balance-of-power concept is simultaneously a highly generalized explanation for the outbreak of conflict and an idea in the heads of individual historical actors in specific situations – such as Sir Edward Grey, the British Foreign Secretary, and Theobald von Bethmann Hollweg, the German Imperial Chancellor, in 1914, and Neville Chamberlain and Adolf Hitler in 1939.

Exercise   What has been the main historical question since the 1960s concerning the causes of the Second World War? ■

Specimen answer and discussion   For a long time 'Hitler' was sufficient answer to those enquiring as to the causes of World War II, and A. J. P. Taylor's famous study must be credited for broadening the question. In his own words, Taylor's book 'has little to do with Hitler. The vital question [...] concerns Great Britain and France. They had the decision in their hands. It was perfectly obvious that Germany would seek to become a Great Power again; obvious after 1933 that her domination would be of a peculiarly barbaric sort. Why did the victors not resist her?' (Taylor, *The Origins of the Second World War*, 1964, p.9). In particular, we must consider the responsibility of Chamberlain both in respect of his overt pursuit of a policy of 'appeasement' in 1938, and for his more problematical policy in 1939. D. C. Watt describes Chamberlain as 'after Hitler ... perhaps the single most important individual in the events of 1939' (Watt, *How War Came*, 1990, p.76). □

Exercise   Having considered why Britain and France decided to resist Germany in 1939, how do you account for their failure to do so earlier? ■

Specimen answer and discussion

France, though it remained Europe's foremost military power until the later 1930s, was gravely weakened by a chronically low birth-rate and the huge losses of young men during World War I. Its pre-eminent foreign policy concern was for security against Germany, a state whose industrial and demographic resources were clearly superior to those of France, and whose relative strength in central and eastern Europe had actually increased with the collapse of Austria-Hungary and Russia and the 'Balkanization' of that region. France regarded strict adherence to the Versailles Treaty as essential to its security, but the failure of the Ruhr occupation in 1923 undermined its will to enforce the treaty single-handedly, caused it to look still more to Britain to guarantee its frontiers, and drew it into a defensive strategic mentality. By stages, France conceded the initiative to Britain in coping with the 'German problem'. The Treaty of Locarno (1925), though it guaranteed France's eastern frontiers and reaffirmed the de-militarization of the Rhineland, was a French diplomatic defeat because it left Germany's eastern frontiers open to revision, and so threatened the integrity of Czechoslovakia and Poland, France's allies. As long as the 'spirit of Locarno' lasted, many French people could convince themselves that war in western Europe was a thing of the past; Aristide Briand, Foreign Minister at this time, is remembered as an apostle of European political unity and '*le pèlerin de la paix*' – the pilgrim of peace. □

The rise of Nazi Germany was immediately recognized as a threat to European stability and peace. No one demanded the revision of Versailles more vehemently than Hitler. But France's ability to respond to this threat was much weakened by the Great Depression, which hit it later than it did other economies, but from which it recovered more slowly, and by its chronic political instability, manifested most acutely in savage riots in February 1934, which threatened the integrity of the state. A small minority of French fascists or neo-fascists welcomed the Nazi regime as a bulwark against Bolshevism; many considered Léon Blum, the French socialist leader of Jewish origin, no less an enemy of the 'real' Catholic, conservative France than Hitler. Despite these weaknesses and divisions, in 1935 France attempted to secure herself against Nazi aggression by allying with the only continental power capable of defeating a rearmed Germany: the Soviet Union. But largely because of French deference to British hostility towards the Soviet Union, the alliance was not followed up by a military convention, or even serious military discussions. The pact gave Hitler a pretext for repudiating Locarno and remilitarizing the Rhineland in 1936; and, although French leaders fully appreciated the strategic significance of Hitler's move, they were paralysed in their response to it by their defensive 'Maginot mentality', their military unpreparedness and their dependence on the British.

Since 1919, many in Britain had come to consider the Versailles settlement morally invalid and politically and economically inept. This 'conventional wisdom' had a corrosive effect on Britain's will to enforce the treaty. It was seen as invalid because it denied to people identifying themselves as German the national self-determination which was supposed to be the treaty's legitimating principle. Since many believed that chief responsibility for the war (into which the nations 'had stumbled', as Lloyd George put it in his *War Memoirs* (1938), once the outrage of the immediate post-war years had subsided) lay in the old diplomatic system of secret diplomacy, the settlement was now also regarded as unjust in pinning sole guilt for the war on Germany. It was politically inept to imagine that such a potentially strong state as Germany would long tolerate the limitations on its forces or the demilitarization of the Rhineland, or to think that in an age of nationalism it would not advance claims on Austria, the Sudetenland and Danzig, where, if given the choice, the majority would choose unification with Germany. It was economically inept to impose a reparations burden on one of the world's leading economies if this hindered the revival of international trade. Such was the case for 'appeasing' Germany.

Germany's main claims before and after 1933 were confined to continental Europe, and British political leaders regarded them with a greater degree of detachment than could the French. Britain was not a continental power, had traditionally avoided continental diplomatic entanglements, and quickly abandoned the conscript army required if it were to play a military role in Europe. What military strength Britain had was further dissipated by the fact that its primary foreign interests were imperial. The peace settlement gave the illusion of being the zenith of Britain's empire, for Britain acquired former German colonies and became the mandate authority in Palestine. However, Britain lacked the military and financial strength needed to meet its imperial commitments, which for long led it to regard states other than Germany as greater potential enemies. Fascist Italy threatened the British presence in the Middle East, and its enmity was assured after Britain concerted the unsuccessful international opposition to the invasion of Abyssinia. The expansion of Japan threatened Britain's position in the Far East.

British leaders, like the French, were answerable to a public opinion in which the memory of the last war was fresh, anxiety about a future war was acute, and 'campaigning' for peace (by the Peace Pledge Union and other groups) was effective. They had good evidence that rearmament was electorally unpopular, and their Treasury officials were convinced it was unaffordable. Very few in Britain opposed the 'appeasement' of Germany; most supported it as apparently the only way to preserve international peace; some welcomed a strong Germany as a bulwark against Bolshevism. Hitler's remilitarization of the Rhineland was not seen at the time in Britain for what it was – a devastating blow at what was left of the Versailles settlement, or if it was, it was welcomed: the Germans were 'only going into their own back garden'. Opinion in France was more realistic: the threat to peace was recognized; but opinion across the political spectrum was fearful of taking any action that might lead to war.

British Conservative leaders had a strong distaste for co-operation with the Soviet Union, and even in 1939, when war was imminent, were extraordinarily dilatory in pursuing a Soviet alliance. Without such an alliance, the military-strategic obstacles to direct, effective resistance to Nazi expansionism were insurmountable. Except for the remilitarization of the Rhineland, all Hitler's moves were made in central and eastern Europe. For France and Britain effectively to oppose Hitler's moves in the Rhineland, Austria, the Sudetenland and Poland would have meant a swift invasion of Germany, which they were not equipped for, had not planned and did not contemplate. Their strategic thinking was geared to a long war of blockade during which they hoped their superior economic resources would slowly wear Germany down (or encourage the emergence of a more tractable regime). Since such a strategy could do nothing in the short term for the victims of Nazi aggression, the British and French were loath to adopt it on the victims' behalf.

Exercise   Why, then, did they eventually oppose Hitler? ∎

Specimen answer and discussion   Not because they regarded Poland as more deserving of support than Czechoslovakia, but because they saw it as in their interests to do so. An unopposed attack on Poland would have left Britain and France passive spectators to Germany's total domination of central and eastern Europe. After the German–Soviet pact, Hitler was assured of an ally in the east which loyally fulfilled its obligations to supply Nazi Germany with war *matériel*. At some point in the future Hitler would have been able to turn on France with overwhelming force and without fear of a war on two fronts. To oppose him in September 1939 – rather than face his attack at some future date – made sense to the western powers because they had been rapidly rearming and believed that the balance of force was more favourable to them now than it would be later. Their intelligence services led them to believe that the German economy was weaker than was actually the case, and would be further undermined by blockade and economic warfare, as in World War I; that Hitler's dictatorship was less secure than it turned out to be; and that the Nazi regime might be toppled from within. Their own economies were dangerously overstretched by rearmament. As democratic states with independent labour movements, they could not (unlike Nazi Germany) contemplate all the measures needed to sustain a 'war economy' without actually being at war. Moreover, in March 1939 a great revulsion of public opinion had followed the German occupation of the vestigial Czech state. While Chamberlain's guarantee to Poland failed to deter Hitler, nearly everyone felt that Hitler 'had to be stopped' and the declaration of war in September was supported by a wide consensus in both Britain and France. □

The Thirty Years' War thesis: for

Book 3, Unit 19 discusses the thesis that the two wars were really a single conflict. It is a familiar argument: Churchill prefaced his book *The Second World War* with the claim that it formed a continuation of the history of World War I which he had set out in *The World Crisis*: 'Together, they cover an account of another Thirty Years' War', with the interwar years as a mere interlude – 'the twenty-year armistice' (Churchill, *The Second World War*, 1967).

Exercise   Can you suggest some arguments in favour of the Thirty Years' War thesis? ∎

Specimen answer and discussion   1   The First World War and the Versailles settlement did not provide a final verdict or a lasting settlement, and left the 'German problem' unresolved. In November 1918 Germany's armies still occupied parts of Belgium, France and above all the former Russian empire, from Finland to the Ukraine and the Caspian. Germany's military and political leaders did not, as in 1945, surrender unconditionally, but requested an armistice. These circumstances lent colour to the impression that Germany's armies had been 'undefeated on the battlefield' and had been forced by the cracking of the 'home front' to accept a truce. This legend of the 'stab in the back' encouraged nationalists to lay the blame for the humiliation of a dicated peace on the Weimar regime. In 1918–19, there was little sense in Germany of defeat, but an abiding sense of resentment at Versailles. In the light of future developments one might argue that until Germany experienced decisive military defeat, complete occupation and dismemberment, as it did in 1945, the aberrant nationalism in its political life would not be expunged and the major cause of international conflict in Europe removed.

2   Despite considerable losses under the Treaty of Versailles, Germany retained its political independence and sovereignty, its demographic superiority and its immense economic potential. It survived as 'the *dominant factor* on the Continent of Europe' (Jan Smuts, in *Primary Sources 2: Interwar and World War II*, Document I.20), its predominance actually enhanced by the weakness of its neighbours in an area fragmented, politically and economically, by the war and the peace settlement. After Versailles, Germany was also the most ethnically homogeneous major state on the continent, and its ruling class and pre-war élites remained in positions of authority and influence. Germany thus quickly recovered to fight a 'second round' in 1939 under circumstances more advantageous than those of 1914. We might thus argue that both wars arose as a result of the 'German problem', 'the problem of fitting Germany into the European political system without endangering the independence of other states and the self-determination of other peoples' (H. Bull (ed.) *The Challenge of the Third Reich*, 1986, p.10). The solution attempted at Versailles in 1919 failed. It was 'too mild for its severity' (Jacques Bainville, *Les Conséquences politiques de la paix*, 1995, p.35): that is, it was sufficiently harsh to foment nationalist grievances, but too lenient to destroy Germany's capacity to redress those grievances.

3   From the near identity of the opposing coalitions in the latter phase of each war, one could argue that the wars were fought for the same geopolitical and strategic objectives. German proposals for the economic domination of western Europe as expressed in the 'September Programme' of 1914 were realized in 1940, after the defeat of France.

4   Another argument is that World War I disrupted (and in places destroyed) the political, economic and social systems of Europe, and the Versailles 'settlement' failed to establish a new order in their place, leaving chronic frictions which eventually flared up into renewed war. This argument for the fundamental defectiveness of Versailles has international and socio-political dimensions. Undermining Versailles from the start was the disintegration of the wartime alliance: the failure of the US to ratify the treaty and its withdrawal from European affairs, and the related failure of the British promise in 1919 to guarantee France against future German aggression. This fuelled France's sense of insecurity and aggravated Anglo-French differences over the 'German problem'. Anglo-French dissent on how far to enforce Versailles was fatal to its fulfilment. Having rejected the option of bringing the war to a more visibly decisive conclusion by invading and dismembering Germany in 1918, Britain and France then differed as to how far to enforce the treaty. France favoured military coercion, culminating in the occupation of the Ruhr in 1923; Britain combined a relatively hard line on reparations with a willingness to accept, in the Treaty of Locarno (1925),

the return of a democratic and liberal Germany to great power status and a policy of distancing itself from France and playing the 'honest broker' between France and Germany. Despite a paper guarantee by Britain at Locarno of France's frontier with Germany, there was no formal British commitment to France until 1936 and no military discussions until 1939.

5   With the collapse of the Austro-Hungarian and Tsarist Empires, the peacemakers were confronted with an anarchic international situation in central and eastern Europe. Before 1914, Russia and Austria-Hungary had been a major source of stability in the ethnic patchwork of central and eastern Europe, and Russia, as the counterweight ally of France in the European balance, had also served to deter German aggression. The successor states, with their welter of claims on each other, constituted a region of chronic instability, and neither Czechoslovakia nor Poland, France's main continental allies, could hope to play the role of counter-weight to Germany that had been undertaken by pre-war Russia. About one-fifth of Poland's citizens were not ethnic Poles and one-third of Czechoslovakia's were neither Czechs nor Slovaks (P. M. H. Bell, *The Origins of the Second World War in Europe*, 1997, pp.28–9; see also Book 2, Units 11–13, section 9). In the 1930s German minorities provided recruits for political terrorism and were exploited by Germany to undermine a state from within (notably with Henlein's Sudeten German Nazis in Czechoslovakia). Nor should we neglect the economic defects of Versailles, whose reparations clauses appeared to Keynes to place, in Bell's words, 'an impossible strain on the German economy [during the Weimar Republic], and involve Germany in permanent balance of payment difficulties, because she would be furnishing exports for which she was not paid, or earning foreign exchange which was not for her own use but for the purpose of making reparations payments' (Bell, 1997, p.23). Attempting to enforce reparations exacerbated German inflation, and thus accelerated one of the most socially disruptive processes in twentieth-century advanced societies. □

In sum, these arguments would lead us to believe that the Second World War followed from the causes and defective settlement of the First.

The Thirty Years' War thesis: against

We can envisage many plausible 'might have beens' – or 'counterfactual scenarios', to use the jargon – which might have diminished the threat of a second general European war, or removed it entirely. Churchill described World War II as 'the Unnecessary War'. 'There never was a war more easy to stop', he claimed (*The Second World War*, 1967, p.x). R. A. C. Parker argues that 'if Churchill had controlled British foreign policy, he would have made a "Grand Alliance", to group other European countries round a firm Anglo-French alliance. The alliance would have pledged defence against any German armed attacks. It might have stopped Hitler, or caused moderate Germans to stop him' (*Churchill and Appeasement*, 2000, p.ix). Above all, war might have been prevented if a determined effort had been made to secure an alliance with Russia in 1939. Such speculation is far from pointless if it helps us see (as it sometimes does) the specific operative causes behind particular events.

A more important difference between the wars is revealed, however, if we consider when and how the main military adversaries became engaged in war. From July–August 1914, the coalitions which bore the brunt of the fighting were at war (France, Russia and Britain versus Germany and Austria-Hungary). Although the entry of Turkey into the war in November, that of Italy in May 1915, and that of the US in March 1917 brought important extensions of the conflict, it did not shift the battle front where the outcome of the war would be decided: France and Flanders. By contrast, the main military adversaries in the Second World War (Germany and the Soviet Union) were at peace until June 1941, and the war's decisive battle fronts in Europe were not opened until that time. (Three-quarters of Germany's military casualties occurred on the Russian front.) An explanation of the causes of the First World War which terminates in August 1914 is true to the 'core' realities of the war that followed. An explanation of the Second World War which stops short at September 1939 greatly distorts its 'core' realities.

Furthermore, the similarity of German geopolitical and strategic objectives in the two world wars should not blind us to the differences in the aims and policies pursued by Germany after 1939, which suggest different causes behind World War II. The military defeat of Poland enabled the Nazis to put into effect policies of subjugation and extermination inspired by an ideology which was actually counterproductive in terms of strategic objectives. Poles in the new *Generalgouvernement* were to be 'natives' in the most pejorative, racist sense – unable to own property, form associations, receive education beyond the primary level, or be employed in any managerial capacity. They were to have only Germans as their masters; there was to be no mixture of blood between Germans and Poles, and Polish leaders and intellectuals were to be executed. Nazi rule over Poland was such as to deprive it of economic usefulness to the Germans; a territory which might have been a valuable source of agrarian produce and raw materials became a giant Golgotha (Bell, 1997, p.307). The contrast between the actions of the central powers in eastern Europe in 1914–18 and in 1939–45 is striking. A recent study by V. J. Liulevicius, *War Land on the Eastern Front* (2000), examines German rule in the 'OberOst' region carved out of Lithuania and parts of Poland and Belarus in World War I with a view to eventual annexation to the *Reich*. Here, while military rule was patronizing and strict, it was also inspired by the desire to impose German standards of order, hygiene, education and culture. Hitler later agreed that 'it was we, who in 1918, created the Baltic countries and Ukraine. But nowadays we have no interest in maintaining Baltic States, any more than in creating an independent Ukraine' (quoted in Liulevicius, 2000, p.271). In 1942, SS Chief Heinrich Himmler chillingly confirmed: 'our duty in the East is not Germanization in the former sense of the term, that is, imposing German language and laws upon the population, but to ensure that only people of pure German blood inhabit the East' (quoted in Liulevicius, 2000, p.268). The difference between Poland in 1914–15, when the Polish legions had subordinated themselves to Austria-Hungary and Varsovians had collaborated under German military rule in the *Generalgouvernement*, and of Nazi Germany in 1939, is tragic evidence that this was much more than a 'replay'. As for the Jews of Poland, random killing by the Germans amounted to 16,000 in September and October 1939 alone. The contrast with the German occupation in World War I is attested by the victims themselves. 'We did not expect the Germans to be pro-Jewish', one survivor recalled of himself as a 13-year-old boy in 1939, 'but on the other hand my parents never expected the Germans to be anything but humane and nice people, since they knew them from the First World War and assumed they would be the same' (quoted in Martin Gilbert, *The Boys: Triumph over Adversity*, 1998, p.67). The policy to eliminate Europe's Jews was carried out with unremitting thoroughness from 1941 right throughout the war, even though it was a distraction from the German war effort.

It has been argued in Unit 19 that Hitler's ultimate military objective was (as he confirmed on coming to office in 1933 and frequently repeated) 'the conquest of *Lebensraum* in the east and its ruthless Germanization'. Serious military planning for an attack on Russia began in August 1940, and on 18 December Hitler signed the top-secret directive 'to crush Soviet Russia in a rapid campaign' – Operation Barbarossa. However, these facts do not mean that the twenty-two months between the invasion of Poland and the launching of Barbarossa were simply a lengthy pause while destiny waited in the wings.

For a start, specific frictions arose in these months from German eastward expansion and Soviet westward expansion, which themselves contributed to Hitler's decision to attack Russia: Germany encroached on Finland, Romania and Bulgaria, states which the Soviet Union considered in its sphere of influence. However, we must bear in mind that not all plans are realized, and Hitler had always matched ideological fixity of purpose with strategic and tactical flexibility. There were good reasons why he might have postponed the attack on Russia or even pursued other grandiose goals. While invasion plans were being drawn up in November 1940, he made some efforts to involve the Soviet Union in a grand coalition with Germany, Italy and Japan to break up the British Empire, and instructed Ribbentrop to present Molotov with a draft agreement for dividing the world into spheres of interest. As long as Britain was undefeated, and many of the world's markets closed to Germany, the alliance with the Soviet Union was very advantageous to Hitler. A commercial agreement of February 1940 stipulated that the Soviet Union should provide Germany during the next year with considerable quantities of cereals, oil, cotton and metal ores, and make purchases in third countries of other goods (such as rubber) on Germany's behalf. The Soviet Union fully discharged its obligations and, in return, received industrial and military technology. The agreement was renewed in 1941 and a further agreement signed in April 1941. Economic co-operation was matched by close collaboration between the Gestapo and the NKVD: German communists were handed over from Russia in exchange for Russian *emigrés* and Ukrainians from Germany.

One needs to add, too, that although Stalin's resort to the Nazi–Soviet pact is sometimes justified as buying time to prepare against later Nazi aggression, German invasion plans were something in which he refused to believe and which the Soviet General Staff did little to counter. The first intelligence of Barbarossa reached Stalin (via the US) in January 1941, and further information flowed in during the next six months. He consistently discounted it as an imperialist plot to involve the Soviet Union in a war with Germany. After the conquest of Yugoslavia (April 1941), Stalin acted as if he believed that a policy of total appeasement would ward off a German attack. We can speculate that the course of events would have been different had the Soviet posture towards

Germany been different; if British and French negligence was a contributory cause of the 1939 war, so too was Soviet negligence in ignoring the signs pointing towards the 1941 war.

Exercise   Such brief consideration of events between September 1939 and June 1941 will have indicated that there were certain immediate, local causes of the 'core' conflict in the Second World War to which the Thirty Years' War thesis blinds us. But there are other reasons for scepticism. Can you suggest some? ■

Specimen answer   1   In the mid- and later 1920s, the so-called 'Locarno era', Stresemann
and discussion   displayed great skill as Germany's Foreign Minister in mitigating the terms of the dictated peace by diplomacy and 'finesse'. As a result of his efforts, Germany was recognized as an equal and entered the League of Nations; reparations were scaled down and discontinued in 1932; and Germany became a favoured field for foreign investment. The recovery of Germany's great power status, including enhanced military standing, *Anschluss* with Austria and the creation of a 'Greater Germany' might have continued in peaceful co-operation with Britain and France had it not been for

2   the shattering effect on German domestic politics and international relations of the Great Depression – a major source of discontinuity in world history. All national economies tried to protect themselves by autarky, which accelerated the collapse of world trade – the total value of Europe's trade in 1935 was only two-fifths of what it had been in 1925 – and extreme nationalism was a common political response to the crisis throughout central and eastern Europe.

3   In Germany, the Great Depression 'gave Nazism its opportunity' (Roberts, p.373). It brought to power a movement whose charismatic leader was motivated by a racist vision of the world, and whose declared pre-eminent goals were eastward expansion and the destruction of the Jews. He and his movement exulted in the barbarization of political life and of warfare. As Goebbels declared in 1928: 'We come as enemies! As the wolf bursts into the flock, so we come!' (quoted in David Thomson (ed.) *The New Cambridge Modern History,* vol.12, 1960, p.474). This was true both with regard to liberal democracy in Germany and with regard to Germany's neighbours, especially in the east. Hitler's 'world view' and the dictatorial violence of his methods represented a qualitative leap from Stresemann's gradual revisionism and from German annexationism in and prior to the First World War. Giving his orders on the eve of Barbarossa, Hitler told his officers 'to rid themselves of obsolete ideologies' and called for 'unprecedented, unmerciful and unrelenting harshness' (see *Primary Sources 2: Interwar and World War II*, Document II.1). Hitler committed Germany to rearmament on a scale which caused considerable economic strain and at a pace which could only be continued by wars of plunder. When Marshal Pétain comforted himself that Hitler was only a more unpleasant version of Kaiser Wilhelm, Paul Reynaud replied: 'No: Hitler is Ghengis Khan' (quoted in Bell, *The Origins of the Second World War in Europe*, 1997, p.319). □

In conclusion, you will no doubt agree that there were many continuities linking the two total wars of twentieth-century Europe, but that it is also important to be aware of the differences between the two world wars. Interpreting the Second World War merely as a continuation of the First might ignore these crucial differences and lead to a distorted view of the nature of these wars, and of the governments that fought them. As we have shown above, for example, while it is true to say that in both world wars Germany had war aims which involved expansion in the east, the nature of those aims, and the way Germany went about achieving them, were different.

3 THE QUESTION OF GERMAN GUILT

Of all the combatants of the First World War Germany has most commonly been singled out as bearing the lion's share of the 'guilt' for causing it. The charge was levelled at the peace conference at Versailles: Germany was compelled to agree to the notorious Article 231 by which it accepted responsibility 'for causing all the loss and damage to which the Allied and Associated Governments [had] been subjected as a consequence of the war imposed upon them by the aggression of Germany and her allies'. This clause subsequently caused embarrassment among some of those who had been at Versailles, and arguably it contributed to the policy of 'appeasement' pursued during the 1930s. It also contributed to Hitler's success in winning electoral support during the 1920s and early 1930s; his subsequent actions overturning the Versailles settlement are generally regarded as helping to maintain the continuing support which the Nazi regime enjoyed. The following account by a young German demonstrates the effect of Hitler's foreign policy successes:

> We had all – teachers as well as pupils – been caught up long since in the giddy whirl of the new regime's great successes. The growth of Germany's power impressed us.
>
> The mood in March 1938 was particularly thrilling. I stood in front of the display copy of the local newspaper and read and re-read the news: 'The Greater German Reich has been formed. Austria, the Eastern March, is part of Germany once more!' A gentleman standing by said to me: 'Yes, my boy, you can be proud – we are living in great times!' And I felt this too. We were living in great times, and their creator and guarantor was Hitler. Adolf Hitler, for us, was the impressive Führer figure. We took the picture we were given for the man. This did not prevent us from mimicking the stereotyped openings of his speeches, as a joke. But we awaited each speech with the tingling expectation that he was about to announce a new German success. We were seldom disappointed.
>
> (Hans Günter Zmarslik, 'Einer vom Jahrgang 1922', quoted in Detlev J. K. Peukert, *Inside Nazi Germany*, 1989, p.149)

While the question of German guilt for the war of 1914 had been open to debate, there was no such ambiguity at the end of the Second World War. The victorious Allies deemed Hitler and the Nazi Party responsible for the outbreak of World War II, and in 1945 they embarked on policies of denazification. In the Russian sector this involved eradicating the 'classes' which had supported Hitler, and in the western sectors it meant seeking out former members of the Nazi Party and punishing or re-educating them (see Book 4, Unit 27 for details).

Perhaps it is understandable that the victors will lay the blame on the vanquished, but given the nature of the crimes committed by Germany under National Socialist leadership, there has rarely been any serious attempt to suggest – as has often been the case with the First World War – that all of the major combatants should share the blame for the outbreak of World War II. As far as the German people were concerned, the evidence suggests that their response to the outbreak of war in 1939 was as muted as it was elsewhere in Europe; similarly there was no popular enthusiasm for Operation Barbarossa in June 1941. However, crucially, it has been suggested, by A. J. P. Taylor and Fritz Fischer, for example, that there was a degree of continuity in German policy that contributed to the outbreak of both world wars. Germans in the new Federal Republic found this suggestion particularly difficult to accept and, as we have seen, such arguments have ensured that these historical questions are always also political ones (see Book 1, Unit 5).

In 1951, in a new edition of *The Course of German History* (first published in 1945), A. J. P. Taylor suggested that there was a continuity in the aggressive foreign policy of Germany:

> The German problem has two sides. How can the peoples of Europe be secured against repeated bouts of German aggression? And how can the Germans discover a settled, peaceful form of political existence? The first problem is capable of solution. Germany is in the centre of Europe and had scored repeated successes by playing off her neighbours to east and west. If these neighbours are united, or even reasonably friendly, then the Germans will not harm us nor even themselves. Nowadays the problem is put in a different form: how can we build up Germany as a Great Power and use her as an ally against the Soviet Union without risk of turning against us? The answer to this is also simple: it is not possible, and those who attempt the impossible will sooner or later pay the penalty. It may be that agreement with the Soviet Union is also impossible. The experiment was abandoned after a few months of sceptical effort; the experiment of living with Germany as a Great Power has been tried, with harsh results, for the last half-century.
>
> (Taylor, 1951, p.9)

Ten years later, in *The Origins of the Second World War*, Taylor argued forcefully that the continuity in German foreign policy linked the two wars. The same year saw the publication of Fritz Fischer's *Griff nach der Weltmacht.* This book caused a furore in Germany by suggesting not only that the Kaiser's government had been quite prepared to risk war in pursuit of their general aims in 1914 but, more seriously, that as soon as the war began they were developing plans, already discussed, for large-scale annexations of territory and the creation of a German-dominated new order in Europe (based on the evidence of the 'September-Programme'; see Unit 5). The point was not lost on Taylor, who commented:

> In 1961 a German professor reported the result of his investigations into German war aims. These were indeed 'a blueprint for aggression' or, as the professor called them, 'a grasp at world power': Belgium under German control; the French iron-fields annexed to Germany; the Ukraine to become German; and, what is more, Poland and the Ukraine to be cleared of their inhabitants and to be resettled with Germans. These plans were not merely

the work of the German general staff. They were endorsed by the German foreign office and by 'the good German', Bethmann Hollweg. Hitler, far from transcending his respectable predecessors, was actually being more moderate than they when he sought only *Lebensraum* in the east and repudiated, in *Mein Kampf*, gains in the west. Hitler merely repeated the ordinary chatter of rightwing circles. Like all demagogues, Hitler appealed to the masses. Unlike other demagogues, who sought power to carry out Left policies, Hitler dominated the masses by leftwing methods in order to deliver them to the Right. This is why the Right let him in.

(Taylor, 1964, p.23)

Of course, as you know, this kind of argument for the continuity of an aggressive German foreign policy linking the Second and Third *Reich* has not gone unchallenged.

Exercise   Read the essay by Norman Rich, 'Hitler's foreign policy', in the Course Reader (Chapter 8) and answer the following questions:

1   On what grounds does Rich challenge Taylor's assertion that, with reference to foreign policy, there was little difference between Hitler and 'virtually all Germans'?

2   What does Rich consider to be the important difference between Hitler's treatment of the Slavs and that of his predecessors? And why does he deem this a point worth considering?

3   To what extent does Rich criticize the conclusions of Eberhard Jäckel's book *Hitler in History*? Why does he do so? ■

Specimen answers   1   Rich warns that 'more careful scholars' might be less willing to assume a knowledge of what the Germans did or did not want (something which you should, of course, bear in mind when writing your own essays or examination answers). It is probably true to say that the Versailles settlement provoked resentment in Germany, but it would be difficult to substantiate the argument that 'virtually all Germans' shared Hitler's expansionist aims, or even that previous German diplomats and foreign ministers had shared them; and, as you should have noticed, Rich himself notes inconsistencies in Taylor's comments in this respect.

2   Rich makes the point that while Hitler set out to exterminate the Slavs, his predecessors (and only the example of the Prussian rule of Poland can be deployed as a comparison) sought to Germanize them. The reason for making this comparison is simply to call in question the simplistic assumption that if Germany had won World War I, then the Kaiser's troops and officials would have received similar orders to those of Hitler, and behaved in a similar way to them.

3   Generally speaking Rich agrees with Jäckel's conclusions, but he parts company with him when Jäckel suggests that there was a long-standing tendency in the history of Germany for imperialistic territorial conquest. Rich believes that this kind of 'fundamental forces' argument is profoundly unhistorical because it leads to a concentration only on those events that foreshadowed the Third *Reich*; other important aspects of the nation's past,

which, conceivably, may have been even more significant, are thus ignored or underestimated. Furthermore, this argument suggests that there is nothing individuals or nations can do to escape a preordained fate.

Discussion   In the debate about the continuity in German foreign policy, it is important to try to keep separate two issues that have a tendency to converge:

1   was Germany responsible for the outbreak of war in 1914 and in 1939–41?

2   were German expansionist plans in 1914–18 similar to those of 1939–45?

It is much easier to argue that Germany was responsible for both wars than it is to argue that German expansionist plans were similar in 1914–18 and 1939–45. All that is needed to demonstrate that Germany was responsible for both wars is to show that German policies were designed to alter the status quo, that German decision-makers consciously embarked on paths to achieve their ends that included a readiness to fight wars, and that when their policies got them into a situation in which they had to fight a war, then they went ahead with it. What the precise territorial objectives might have been, and what kind of political order was envisaged after a successful war, are rather different things. Furthermore, it needs to be stressed that while Fischer's arguments addressed the guilt of the decision-makers, he did not raise the question of the guilt of the German people. Again, this distinction needs to be borne in mind when looking at the events of 1939 and 1941, where it becomes contentious because of the distinction that historians (and others) have made between the Nazis and the German people. □

Taylor's book deals with the outbreak of war in 1939. There is some justification for arguing that the war did not become a 'world' war until 1941, with the beginning of Germany's war with Russia and the broadening of the conflict in the Far East. There can be no doubt that a truly titanic struggle was fought on the eastern front between Germany and the USSR. This was the real war as far as many Germans were (and are) concerned. Not surprisingly, some of the most heated historical controversies in recent German history focus on the war against Bolshevism as Nazism's primary enemy.

   In the second half of the 1980s, a number of German historians were advancing arguments which seemed to their opponents akin to heresy. Andreas Hillgruber argued forcefully that the tragedy of World War II was the destruction of central Europe and the advance of Soviet power. For Hillgruber, one of the principal dynamic forces in modern history was national consolidation. However, Germany's attempts to achieve such consolidation had a serious effect on the international system: the numbers of ethnic Germans, the position of the territories they inhabited, and the economic richness of those territories, meant that Germany could not be brought together without dominating the international system in Europe. This potential domination, in turn, produced massive coalitions to prevent it. In *Zweierlei Untergang: die Zerschlagung des Deutschen Reiches und das Ende des Europäischen Judentums* ('Two kinds of demise: the shattering of the German *Reich* and the end of European Jewry'), published in 1986, Hillgruber argued that the atrocities committed by the Red Army, and the fear of such atrocities, justified the ferocious resistance of the German army and also solved the moral dilemma of their fighting to preserve Hitler's Germany. He urged readers to identify with the German soldiers struggling to protect their people and their country against the red hordes intent on rape and plunder, who were enabling many thousands of the inhabitants of the *Reich*'s eastern provinces to escape from Soviet terror.

However, on the other hand, most of the death camps were in the east, and the longer the German army held up the Soviet advance the longer these camps could function. Nazi extermination policy and how to evaluate it, never mind explain how it could happen, is another contentious issue around the question of German 'guilt'. The questions of whether the Holocaust was a singularly horrific event, impossible to compare to any other atrocity, and how much responsibility attaches to 'ordinary' Germans in facilitating this murderous activity, have been debated by historians, politicians, journalists and philosophers. All are anxious to come to terms with Germany's recent history, and particularly with the question of whether or not Hitler and the Nazis were an aberration or something peculiarly and specifically German.

In a controversial study on the question of Nazism, Ernst Nolte argued that fascism was a European phenomenon of which Hitler and the Nazis were only one variant. In Nolte's words, fascism

> is anti-Marxism which seeks to destroy the enemy by the involvement of a radically opposed and yet related ideology and by the use of almost identical and yet typically modified methods, always, however, within the unyielding framework of national self-assertion and autonomy.
>
> (Nolte, *Three Faces of Fascism*, 1965, pp.20–21)

Nolte also suggests that the Holocaust was part and parcel of this development in as much as it was the mirror image of the class murder committed by the Bolsheviks: the European bourgeoisie (a term used by Nolte), terrified of, and threatened by, the Bolsheviks, turned on a part of itself – the Jews.

Nolte's views proved controversial, but they were not widely discussed until 1986, when he published in a national German newspaper an article entitled 'The past that will not pass away' ('Vergangenheit, die nicht vergehen will', *Frankfurter Allgemeine Zeitung*, 6 June 1986). Together with the views of Hillgruber, and those of a third German historian, Michael Stürmer, this appeared to critics to be a right-wing attempt to whitewash German history, to 'relativize' the Holocaust. Nolte proposed that new questions be asked, in particular regarding the singularity of the Holocaust, and its causal connection with crimes committed by the Bolsheviks. In Nolte's words,

> the following question must be deemed admissible, indeed necessary. Did the National Socialists carry out, did Hitler perhaps carry out an 'Asiatic' deed only because they regarded themselves and their kind as potential or real victims of an 'Asiatic' deed? Wasn't the 'Gulag Archipelago' more original than Auschwitz? Wasn't class murder on the part of the Bolsheviks logically and actually prior to race murder on the part of the Nazis?
>
> (Quoted in R. J. B. Bosworth, *Explaining Auschwitz and Hiroshima*, 1993, p.82)

Such controversial statements did not, of course, go unchallenged, either by German or international historians. The ensuing *Historikerstreit* (historians' debate) raised several philosophical problems, but essentially it focused on two historical questions:

1   Was the Nazis' mass murder of Jews, as well as of other minorities and 'deviants', something unique, or can it be compared to other historical examples of mass murder and genocide?

2   Was there a causal connection between mass murder by the Nazis (and the acceptance and involvement of ordinary Germans in the Holocaust) and the actions of the Bolsheviks which predated it? Was the Holocaust perhaps conceived of only after the atrocities committed by the Bolsheviks seemed to make such horrors possible?

Exercise   Turn back to Rich's essay. How does he describe Jäckel's analysis of the Holocaust? ■

Specimen answer   Jäckel does not attempt to exonerate the German people from their support for Hitler and the voluntary obedience of those who carried out his criminal orders. However, he does stress the lack of information available to most Germans in the Nazi period, and he argues that, although Hitler's programme was outlined in *Mein Kampf*, there is no evidence that he was given power simply to implement this programme.

Discussion   Jäckel, like most of his contemporaries, was a participant in the *Historikerstreit*. In particular, he was one of those who pointed out that Nolte's suggestion of a causal connection between mass murder by the Bolsheviks and mass murder by the Nazis was based on the flimsiest of evidence. Jäckel stressed that a considerable amount is now known about the elements that contributed to the way in which Hitler viewed the world and the process of history, and Russian atrocities scarcely figured in this.

It is likely that individual Germans who were fully aware of, and opposed to, the violence and the atrocities of the regime found it difficult to know how and at what point to protest. The Holocaust was a very gradual development in Nazi policy. There seems to have been general support for a tough 'law and order' policy in Germany during the 1930s. The assault on the left which followed the Nazi takeover received widespread approval, and the first of the concentration camps, at Dachau near Munich, which was established in March 1933, was regarded by many non-Nazis as an acceptable way of dealing with 'troublemakers' and 'revolutionaries'. The extermination of Röhm and the SA in 1934 appears to have been accepted on the grounds that Röhm and many of his lieutenants were homosexuals and the SA were thugs; Hitler, many believed, wanted decency in everyday life and this was one way of establishing it. As Detlev Peukert notes:

> Many older people today, looking back on the Third Reich, still see it as having had two strong points in its favour that made up for a lot: people could leave their bicycles unlocked outside their front doors; and long-haired layabouts were hauled off into Labour Camps. Even if such attitudes fell short of a demand for the death penalty or the gas chamber (though these demands were common enough), they testify to the existence of popular consent to a specific form of terror, namely dealing with non-standard behaviour, or non-standard categories of person, by bundling the individuals concerned into camps and subjecting them to drill even if not to annihilation. It should not be

forgotten that a complementary part of the stock folk memory about
unlocked bicycles that were safe against theft was the knowledge that
gypsies were being arrested as 'theft suspects' and imprisoned in
concentration camps.

(Peukert, *Inside Nazi Germany*, 1989, p.198)

The *Reichspogromnacht* of November 1938, in contrast, appears to have
provoked general obloquy among the population and to have ensured that
when the 'Final Solution' began to be implemented in 1941, information about it
was circulated by the authorities with considerable circumspection and caution.
Protest at this point may have been met with disbelief; it may also have been
branded as unpatriotic since the Final Solution began only after the struggle on
the eastern front had also begun.

Like many historical controversies, and particularly those concerned with
modern German history, the *Historikerstreit* was, in Ian Kershaw's words 'in
essence a political discourse'. It was a debate 'about the way the society of the
highly developed, prosperous, and stable Federal Republic can cope with living
with its Nazi past. This is an unending debate in which the expertise of historians
offers no great advantage or special privilege' (Kershaw, quoted in Bosworth,
Explaining Auschwitz and Hiroshima, 1993, p.77).

The *Historikerstreit* abated in 1989, when the two Germanies were reunited
into one democratic state. Given Europe's recent history, there were many
concerned voices, both within and outside Germany, who feared that the new,
larger Germany might once again threaten the peace of Europe, that the
'German question' would once again raise its head. (In Britain, for example,
Prime Minister Margaret Thatcher, who was much opposed to the reunification
of Germany, employed a team of historians to advise her on the probable threat
posed by the new Germany.)

However, reunification did not spell the end of historical controversies in
Germany. The publication of Daniel J. Goldhagen's study *Hitler's Willing
Executioners* in 1996 provoked another public controversy about history,
although one that was more short-lived. Interestingly, while most historians
dismissed Goldhagen's main thesis of the inherent anti-Semitic nature of 'the
Germans' and of the implication of 'ordinary Germans' in the Holocaust, most
'ordinary Germans' were convinced by Goldhagen's arguments and were only
too willing to accept his devastating thesis (and helped to turn the book into an
almost unprecedented publishing success). Even more impact was made by
another public debate about Germany's history, this time sparked off by a
controversial exhibition. The exhibition detailed the war crimes and atrocities
committed by the German *Wehrmacht* against civilians on the eastern front, in
Yugoslavia and Greece. Up to this point it had generally been believed by the
public (although not by historians) that only the SS had been responsible for war
crimes and atrocities – the post-war image of the '*saubere Wehrmacht*' (the
'clean army') had been one untainted by the horrors of Nazism. The political
nature of historical questions was, once again, emphasized by the very public
nature of the debate, and by the fact that special debates took place in the

Bundestag to try to resolve this heated controversy. So what exactly were Germans arguing about? The journalist Hans-Günther Thiele summed it up as follows:

> German guilt regarding the outbreak of the Second World War is undisputed among the democrats in this country, and undisputed, too, are the crimes that were committed by Germans during that time, including the murder of the European Jews. We also do not dispute that part of the *Wehrmacht* took part in these crimes, large parts, directly and indirectly.
>
> But we do, for example, argue over whether the *Wehrmacht*, based on today's knowledge, should be regarded as a criminal organization, how we should evaluate the role of military resistance to Hitler, whether after the war the myth of the 'clean *Wehrmacht*' took root, and whether the *Bundeswehr* bears a birthmark because its first officers had sworn an oath of allegiance to Hitler.
>
> (Hans-Günther Thiele (ed.) *Die Wehrmachtsausstellung*, 1997, pp.8–9; my translation)

Many difficult questions about the people and their history continue to occupy the German nation. In many ways, as long as the questions raised by the Fischer controversy and by the *Historikerstreit* continue to haunt Germany's 'national conscience', the nation's troubled and traumatic past cannot be consigned to history. □

References

Abelshauser, W. (1998) 'Germany: guns, butter, and economic miracles', in Harrison, M. (ed.) *The Economics of World War II*, Cambridge University Press.

Bainville, J. (1995) *Les Conséquences politiques de la paix*, Editions de l'Arsenal (first published 1919).

Barber, J. and Harrison, M. (1991) *The Soviet Home Front 1941–1945: A Social and Economic History of the USSR in World War II*, Longman.

Bell, P. M. H. (1997) *The Origins of the Second World War in Europe*, 2nd edn, Longman.

Berghahn, V. R. (1987) *Modern Germany: Society, Economy and Politics in the Twentieth Century*, 2nd edn, Cambridge University Press.

Boog, H. *et al.* (1998) *Germany and the Second World War*, vol.4, *The Attack on the Soviet Union*, Clarendon Press.

Bosworth, R. J. B. (1993) *Explaining Auschwitz and Hiroshima: History Writing and the Second World War 1945–1990*, Routledge.

Bull, H. (ed.) (1986) *The Challenge of the Third Reich*, Clarendon Press.

Churchill, W. S. (1967) *The Second World War*, vol.1, *The Gathering Storm*, Cassell (first published 1948).

Craig, G. A. (1981) *Germany 1866–1945*, Oxford University Press.

Erickson, J. (1983) *The Road to Berlin: Stalin's War with Germany*, vol.2, Weidenfeld and Nicolson.

Fest, J. C. (1974) *Hitler*, Weidenfeld and Nicolson.

Förster, J. (1998) 'Operation Barbarossa as a war of conquest and annihilation', in Boog, H. *et al.*, *Germany and the Second World War*, vol.4, *The Attack on the Soviet Union*, Clarendon Press.

Förster, S. (1995) 'Der deutsche Generalstab und die Illusion des kurzen Krieges, 1871–1914: Metakritik eines Mythos', *Militärgeschichtliche Mitteilungen*, vol.54, no.1, pp.61–98.

Gattrell, P. and Harrison, M. (1993) 'The Russian and Soviet economies in two world wars: a comparative view', *Economic History Review*, vol.XLVI, no.3, pp.425–52.

Gilbert, M. (1983) *Finest Hour: Winston S. Churchill 1939–1941*, Heinemann.

Gilbert, M. (1998) *The Boys: Triumph over Adversity*, Phoenix.

Goldhagen, D. J. (1996) *Hitler's Willing Executioners: Ordinary Germans and the Holocaust*, Alfred A. Knopf.

Harrison, M. (1998) 'The economics of World War II: an overview', in Harrison, M. (ed.) *The Economics of World War II*, Cambridge University Press.

Hoffmann, P. (1998) 'The conduct of the war through Soviet eyes', in Boog, H. *et al.*, *Germany and the Second World War*, vol.4, *The Attack on the Soviet Union*, Clarendon Press.

Israel, J. I. (1982) *The Dutch Republic and the Hispanic World 1606–1661*, Clarendon Press.

Liulevicius, V. J. (2000) *War Land on the Eastern Front: Culture, National Identity and German Occupation in World War I*, Cambridge University Press.

Lloyd George, D. (1938) *War Memoirs*, Odhams.

Mann, M. (1993) *The Sources of Social Power*, vol.2, *The Rise of Classes and Nation-States, 1760–1914*, Cambridge University Press.

Marwick, A. (2001) *The New Nature of History: Knowledge, Evidence, Language*, Macmillan.

Milward, A. S. (1977) *War, Economy and Society, 1939–1945*, Allen Lane.

Moore, Barrington, Jr (1966) *Social Origins of Dictatorship and Democracy: Lord and Peasant in the Making of the Modern World*, Allen Lane.

Müller, R. D. (1998) 'The failure of the economic "Blitzkrieg Strategy"', in Boog, H. *et al.*, *Germany and the Second World War*, vol.4, *The Attack on the Soviet Union*, Clarendon Press.

Nolte, E. (1965) *Three Faces of Fascism: Action Française, Italian Fascism, National Socialism*, Weidenfeld and Nicolson.

Overy, R. J. (1995) *Why the Allies Won*, Jonathan Cape.

Overy, R. J. (1998) *Russia's War*, Allen Lane.

Parker, R. A. C. (2000) *Churchill and Appeasement*, Macmillan.

Peukert, D. J. K. (1989) *Inside Nazi Germany: Conformity, Opposition and Racism in Everyday Life*, Penguin.

Purdue, A. W. (1999) *The Second World War*, Macmillan.

Taylor, A. J. P. (1951) *The Course of German History*, Hamish Hamilton (first published 1945).

Taylor, A. J. P. (1964) *The Origins of the Second World War*, Penguin (first published 1961).

Thiele, H.-G. (ed.) (1997) *Die Wehrmachtsausstellung. Dokumentation einer Kontroverse*, Edition Temmen.

Thomson, D. (ed.) (1960) *The New Cambridge Modern History*, vol.12, *The Era of Violence 1898–1945*, Cambridge University Press.

Turner, H. A., Jr (1975) 'Fascism and modernization', in Turner, H. A., Jr (ed.) *Reappraisals of Fascism*, New Viewpoints.

Walzer, M. (1980) *Just and Unjust Wars*, Penguin.

Watt, D. C. (1990) *How War Came: The Immediate Origins of the Second World War, 1938–1939*, Mandarin (first published 1989).

Wehler, H. U. (1979) Introduction to *Imperialism*, in Emsley, C. (ed.) *Conflict and Stability in Europe*, Croom Helm.

Wright, Q. (1942) *A Study of War*, 2 vols, University of Chicago Press.

Unit 29 THE PROCESSES OF CHANGE

ARTHUR MARWICK, BILL PURDUE, MARK PITTAWAY
AND BERNARD WAITES

(Section 1 by Arthur Marwick; section 2 by Bill Purdue; section 3 by Mark Pittaway; section 4 by Bernard Waites)

Open University students of this unit will need to refer to:

Course Reader: *Total War and Historical Change: Europe 1914–1955*, eds Clive Emsley, Arthur Marwick and Wendy Simpson, Open University Press, 2000

1   ASSUMPTIONS AND THEORIES

Apart from assessing how well you have profited from the various resources we have provided you with in this course, the exam is also a test of how effective our teaching material has been – of, in fact, how well we have taught you. The exam springs out of *what* we have taught you, and the *way* in which we have taught it. Unlike some courses you may have studied, ours has not been filled with theory. But that does not mean that it has been a brainless course, a course lacking in intellectual challenge, a course in which you do not need to do a great deal of thinking.

In Book 1, Unit 1, and in the *Residential School Booklet*, having first asked you to reflect on the immense amount of change which took place in Europe between 1914 and 1955, I then asked you to think about explanations for this. Now there are grand theories of change, in particular Marxism, which envisage change coming about through a lower class coming into conflict with, and eventually overthrowing, the dominant class. That theory has found no place in this course. However, one might feel some sympathy with the broadly Marxist view that material, or economic, factors are the governing, or at least the most important, ones in bringing about change. But then many historians have argued that demographic factors (birth-rates, death-rates, population change in general) are the most important ones. I have suggested tackling economic and demographic factors together, along with technological ones, thus speaking of 'structural' factors, or circumstances. (I say 'circumstances' because low levels of economic and technological development and adverse demographic conditions can *inhibit* change as well as advance it.) We can't stop there: for historians now recognize too that thoughts, ideas, beliefs (what I have referred to as 'ideological' circumstances) can be forces for change (as well as forces inhibiting change).

One could have a *theory* that at all times structural factors are more important than ideological ones. But it would not be a very useful theory. Sometimes ideological circumstances clearly are paramount in bringing about certain specific changes; it is best, I would say, to study the way structural and ideological forces interact with each other. Then we have 'institutional' circumstances (churches, parliaments, trade unions, etc.). Different types of institutions in different countries can be at least part of the explanation for different rates of change in these countries. This is perhaps less a theoretical, or even conceptual approach, than simply a way of organizing information: if you find it helpful, use it – but if you find it cumbersome and confusing, forget it.

What *is* required in an exam answer is some attempt at organizing your material. It is not enough just to let all the facts you can think of tumble out: you must offer analysis, explanation, interpretation. A central concern of this course is that of how far the wars themselves, compared with other forces and agents of change, were responsible for the transformations that we can identify between 1914 and 1955. Obviously there are processes of change taking place irrespective of the wars. It is the purpose of this book to discuss these. It will be your task in many of your exam questions to balance the long-term processes of change against such effects (if any) as were brought about by the wars. I suppose I have come very close to producing a theory (though a very limited and specific one) in arguing that to pin down what changes we can attribute to

structural

×

ideological

wars, we should compare the processes in play in 'society not at war' with those in play in 'society at war'. I have then gone further in trying to sort out the latter under four headings: destruction and disruption; testing of and stress placed upon existing institutions; participation of underprivileged groups; cataclysmic psychological experience. But again these are to be used only if useful and relevant, and not if not.

Marxism had a theory about how revolutions came about quite independently of war: the newly rising class rose up to overthrow the existing ruling class. However, that leading Marxist in the Russian revolution, Leon Trotsky, declared that 'war is the locomotive of history'. We certainly couldn't have a theory that total wars always bring revolutions, and I don't think we could even have one that wars are essential to revolutions (that is to say, if there is no war there will be no revolution). The political scientist Hannah Arendt produced the theory that defeat in war led to revolution. Mention this by all means in your exam answers, but, of course, as is usually the case in history, just stating the theory isn't really very helpful. What you have to do is identify the various causes of the particular revolution you are dealing with, and decide what weighting, if any, to give to the particular war during, or at the end of, which the revolution took place.

You do need to have a certain conceptual background if you are to handle the question of class adequately. The course material advises caution in accepting that there is a clearly defined bourgeoisie which, after overthrowing the aristocracy, has become the undisputed ruling class. The class structures of east Europe and west Europe are rather different. The notion that at any time there are just two competing classes is not to be entered on lightly. You should understand the (different) views of Arno J. Mayer and Charles S. Maier, but you should understand too why they have been criticized in the units, particularly by John Golby, but also by Bill Purdue and myself. When you come into the exam, be sure that you have clear views about class worked out in your own mind: if you are not sure, do not attempt any question in which the word 'class' appears.

You may find it useful to make a distinction between the nationalism of the submerged nationalities seeking a nation state of their own, and the nationalism of the established nation states. Britain and France were the long-established ones, but Germany and Italy (with some territory still 'missing') had become ones by 1914. There are theories about nationalism being entirely invented, or imagined, or constructed, and about nationalism being essentially a political movement rather than something determined by ethnic identity. As long as you grasp the significance of nationalism, and the separate nationalisms, as both are expounded in the units, then there is no need to go into these theoretical issues.

Other words or phrases which may be associated with particular theories are 'total war' and 'totalitarianism'. Both the first and the last chapters in your Course Reader give reasons for arguing that 'total war' is not an entirely appropriate label for the First and Second World Wars. With regard to the military aspects of the wars (and, after all, wars are essentially military events) these may well not really have been total wars; certainly they did not entirely coincide with nineteenth-century theories about what a real total war would involve. Total control of civilians, of the home fronts, was never achieved by any government in either of the wars. However, phrases such as 'total war' are generally used by historians in a comparative, relative manner. Compared with earlier (and some later) wars the ramifications at home and on all aspects of life were immense. To term a war a 'total war' is not to answer a question, but only to open an enquiry: we still have to work out the detail, the ramifications, recognizing the areas where control was very far from total. For the purposes of this course it is suggested that you use the term 'total war' as a broadly descriptive one, implying that (as compared with previous wars) it really is worth studying what happened on the home front, without, however, predetermining any conclusions that might be arrived at.

Similar things might be said about 'totalitarianism'. At most, we can use it as a broad descriptive category to link together those countries which had one-party dictatorships, most notably Russia, Germany and Italy, and to distinguish them from those countries which had liberal democratic governments, most notably Britain and France. During the height of the Cold War very rigid definitions were developed by right-wing American political scientists (subjected to some criticism in Book 3, Unit 16 on Mussolini's Italy by Geoffrey Warner): but one can accept 'totalitarianism' as a useful label (as indeed Warner does) without having to accept the rigid definitions. What recent work has been pointing to is that there were many limits on how totalitarian (that is, how total in its control of the population) a government actually could be. It is important that you should be aware of this latest work: but the main thing is that, if you use the term 'totalitarian', you are absolutely clear and explicit about how you are using it.

This takes us to the term 'revisionist'. Those who have recently been writing about certain regimes, helped by the primary source materials which became available after the fall of the Soviet Union in 1989, are, within that particular field of specialization, known as 'revisionists'. 'Revisionist' is not a general term for a particular type of historian (unlike, say, 'Marxist', or 'feminist'). If you are using the term, be clear that it refers to a particular group of historians within a particular field of study.

Throughout the course, in referring to individual historians associated with a notable interpretation of a particular topic, we have tended to speak of their 'thesis' rather than their 'theory' ('thesis' also has another entirely separate meaning, sometimes being used instead of 'dissertation' to describe the end product of someone working on a PhD): thus we have the Fischer thesis, the Maier thesis, perhaps the A. J. P. Taylor thesis. It is not absolutely vital to bring in the views of such historians, but if you are aiming for a good mark we expect you, when dealing with the origins of the First World War, say, to bring in Fischer; when dealing with the effects of that same war on class, to bring in Maier; and when dealing with the origins of the Second World War, to bring in Taylor. Or you may get questions specifically directing you to discuss 'the Fischer thesis', 'the Maier thesis', etc. In either case, you must be completely sure that you do fully understand the arguments put forward by the particular historian. Do not attempt any question mentioning the specific name of a historian if you are not clear about this; and do not start dropping the names of historians in more general questions unless you really can knowledgeably back up what you are saying.

The assumptions behind all this are the assumptions of most professional historians: that the events, developments and changes which took place in Europe between 1914 and 1955, and which are discussed in this course, though they are now past and gone for good, did have a real existence; and, further, that through the primary sources left to us from that period, we can engage with these events, developments and changes. We assume, too, that the secondary sources by historians that we have recommended to you are reliable, well-founded and as objective as it is possible for fallible human beings to be. That is our 'theory' of history, though, as I said in Unit 1, I think it is better to speak of 'assumptions'.

I imagine you will have little difficulty with these assumptions. Through studying other subjects, however, you may be familiar with the latest postmodernist theories about how historians simply tell a variety of stories and about how they are, in any case, governed by the 'narrative' form in which they write. If this is the case, I hope you have found sufficient in this course to persuade you that historians are very reflexive about their methods, that they are justified in believing that their methods do result in genuine contributions to our knowledge of the past, and that, indeed, they do have arguments with which to counter those put forward by the postmodernists. In a history exam, it is best to conform to the assumptions of historians, leaving all grand-scale theory outside the exam room. In practical terms, this means that you should address directly the questions you are asked, giving as much specific evidence as you can for your clear but balanced arguments. Do not waste time on developing some grand theory or generalization. Remember that sometimes within one question there are contained several separate questions. Always be sure to break the question down into its component parts, and then be sure that you have given an answer to each of these component parts.

2 SOCIAL CHANGE 1914–1955

As Arthur Marwick has suggested, social change 'is not rigidly distinguished from other sorts of historical change, but is indeed seen as embracing, or being closely involved with them' (Unit 1, p.5). Rather than worry too much about where the dividing lines are between social change and cultural, political or economic change, we should treat the term 'social' as denoting the emphasis rather than the precise content. We should also try to look coolly at 'change', an objective word, which is too often elided into 'progress'. The first half of the twentieth century saw plenty of changes but whether for the better or the worse is another matter.

Change and continuity

One of the great historical clichés is to write that 'it was an age of change'. Weren't they all? Well, up to a point. There have been periods, certainly half-centuries, in human history when, for the great majority, life must have changed very little: periods at the end of which essentially the same technology was available as at the beginning; employment and work patterns were much the same, as were social and political structures, while cultural and religious attitudes remained little changed. Although rapid change is by no means confined to recent history (imagine, for instance, living at the beginning or end of the Roman Empire, or in east-central Europe when the Ottoman Turks were invading), it can be argued that technological and economic development has meant that rapid change has been almost the norm for the late modern period.

The other great cliché, or as Marwick has put it, 'platitude', is that history is concerned with both continuity and change. It is perhaps less of a platitude to point to the disposition of historians writing at different periods to stress one rather than the other. Think, for example, of the different ways in which European society before 1914 has been interpreted. For a long time pre-1914 society, in western Europe at any rate, was portrayed as essentially (to use Marxist terminology) *bourgeois* – a society in which real power had passed from landowning aristocracies to businessmen, bankers or industrialists. This was for long enough the picture painted not only by Marxists but also, though they have used different terminology, by most historians who, if they depicted a complex society where considerable power and influence was held by kings and aristocrats, nevertheless emphasized the emergence of a new order, a 'modern' society. Writing in 1981, however, Arno J. Mayer, although a Marxist, emphasized continuity rather than change:

> For too long historians have focused excessively on the advance of science and technology, of industrial and world capitalism, of the bourgeoisie and professional middle class, of liberal civil society, of democratic political society, and of cultural modernism. They have been far more preoccupied with these forces of innovation and the making of a new society than with the forces of inertia and resistance that slowed the waning of the old order.
>
> (Mayer, *The Persistence of the Old Regime*, 1981, p.4)

Mayer's view represented an historical trend, an increased emphasis upon continuity, which became pronounced in the late twentieth century. Associated with this was a tendency to see change as gradual, steady and guided by tenacious tradition. Revolutions and great watersheds – the very stuff of histories written in the 1960s – were progressively downgraded in importance. Indeed one prominent historian, writing of British history, complained that all the interesting bits of historical landscape, the hills and the valleys, were being replaced by a flat plain, 'humdrum happenings rather than high drama' (David Cannadine, 'British history: past, present and future', 1987).

The development of Russian society in the twentieth century provides another example of how interpretations can differ depending on whether the emphasis is on change or continuity. We might emphasize change, and thus see it as the consequence of a great cataclysmic event, the Bolshevik Revolution, which inaugurated a great social experiment. Or we might, as Richard Pipes does, emphasize continuity, highlighting the absence of a tradition of private property in Tsarist Russia as providing a ready basis for a totalitarian regime (*Russia Under the Bolshevik Regime 1919–24*, 1994). Along similar lines, we might explain Britain's post World War II social welfare legislation as the consequence of the effects of World War II; or we might argue that it was a continuation of the trajectory of Neville Chamberlain's interwar social legislation; or we might even see it as part of a consistent line of development from the pre-1914 legislation.

Questions of change and continuity have clear implications for our concern with total war and social change. It seems more than likely that even without two major wars Europe would have experienced considerable social change between 1914 and 1955. After all, between 1850 and 1914 and between 1955 and

2000 there were no major wars in Europe but in both periods European societies were much altered, even transformed. A question worth asking yourself is whether social structures, attitudes, beliefs and ways of life changed more, or less, between 1914 and 1955 than they did between 1955 and 2000. However, even if you decide that social change was greater between 1955 and 2000, and so take the view that the two total wars were of less importance than other factors in instigating change, this would only qualify any thesis posing a relationship between war and social change because:

(a) no argument we consider in this course suggests that war is the major cause of social change;

 (b) it could well be that the effects of the world wars continued to be vital long after the wars were over;

 (c) the essential debates are about whether the wars speeded up change, slowed down change, made no difference in the long term or deflected and altered the paths of change.

A further point is that, across Europe as a whole, neither continuity nor change was even. Someone born in Slovakia in 1914 would by the mid-1950s have lived, without moving home, in the Austro-Hungarian Empire, the Czechoslovakian Republic, a nominally independent Slovakia and Czechoslovakia again. (By 2000 a nonagenarian would have been living in another Slovakia.) The British not only escaped such geopolitical changes, but were by mid-century living in much the same mature industrial society, with a very similar social structure, as the one in which they had lived in 1914. (The great changes to the British economy, culture and society were to come in the second half of the century.)

What we are concerned with is both charting change and evaluating 'the significance of war as against all the other possible factors' (Unit 1, p.13). This course has given you many questions, a lot of information, some possible explanations but little in the way of definite answers. What we hope it has done is to get you to think about the processes of change.

Change over time

Historians tend to divide into those who hold to broad theories to explain historical development and those who belong to a more empirical tradition. The distinction is not, however, a hard and fast one. In the end all historians, even those who eschew grand theories, have to generalize, while those committed to broad theories of change have to modify them when confronted by awkward facts or by particular developments. Many historians incorporate elements of both approaches. Certainly all historians attempt to explain why certain things happened; we can, however, distinguish different ranks of explanation, from the specific ('World War I led to the fall of the Kaiser'), to the theory of limited range ('defeat in war leads to revolution'), to the holistic ('class struggle is the motor of history').

Among the categories of factors promoting change, Unit 1 introduced the concept of structural forces. Broad historical theories tend to suggest that certain basic developments or even constants are the prime factors determining change. Traditional Marxist approaches stress long-term economic change and its effect in displacing or creating social classes. More recent Marxist approaches and those of many non-Marxist historians give a more independent role to other factors, such as social attitudes or culture, but remain wedded to the idea of an overall pattern of structural forces with economic development in a privileged position as the instrument of change. There are, however, other structural approaches, such as those which, over the long term, assign prime importance to geographic factors. Halford Mackinder, the leading British geopolitical thinker at the beginning of the twentieth century, saw Europe and European history as subordinate to Asia and Asiatic history in that it was the history of a long struggle with Asiatic invasions ('The geographical pivot of history', 1904).

In opposition to structural factors are contingent factors. In Unit 1 Arthur Marwick defined 'contingency' as 'chance event or occurrence'. Given its unpredictability, we can perhaps see the weather as contingent. The failure of Operation Barbarossa clearly had an important impact upon the future course of European history; among the reasons for its failure were the atrocious winters of the early 1940s. The spring and early summer of 1941 saw cold and wet weather, which delayed the start of the German invasion, while the winter of 1941–42 saw exceptionally low temperatures and heavy snowfalls. (Hitler's weather experts had forecast that the winter of 1941–42 would be a mild one.) Coal and food shortages in the dire winter of 1947 certainly played a part in denting the reputation of the post-war Labour government in Britain. Another example of contingency is the absence of the US aircraft-carriers from Pearl Harbor on 7 December 1941. If this was indeed by chance, then American good fortune played its part in the progress of the Pacific War.

The outcome of wars and why one side won rather than another provides an interesting case study for the relative importance of long-term structural factors as opposed not just to chance but to decisions made by governments, high commands and individuals. Richard Overy in an important book, *Why the Allies Won* (1995), has challenged the widely accepted thesis that, once the US and the USSR were in the war, an Allied victory was virtually inevitable. The balance of strength was against the Axis: any addition of the industrial productivity and size of populations of the Allies as opposed to the Axis comes down heavily in favour of the former. This concept of the inevitability of Allied victory is essentially based upon an elevation of economic strength and resources over military decisions and the outcome of battles. In Overy's view, we need to consider not just the resources of home economies but the potential and use made of the economies of conquered territories, the decisions of generals, the performance of armed forces, and the choices made as to the development and production of weaponry. The reasons for the Allied victory lay in the mistakes of the Axis powers as well as the strengths of the Allies.

Another term or concept that challenges the broad theories or the supremacy of structural factors is the particular. Grand generalizations are always challenged by claims that particular instances don't bear them out. Are particular characteristics of nations and societies unimportant and largely explained by different stages of development within a broad pattern of economic and social change, or are they firmly grounded in past experiences? Consider the particular differences between Poland and Czechoslovakia in the 1930s, their economies, social structures, and political and religious traditions. Do we explain Czechoslovakia's greater degree of liberal democracy as a result of structural factors (because Czechoslovakia had a more industrialized economy, for example) or as a result of the two nations' distinct historical traditions? Did the decision of the Czechs not to fight in 1938 and the decision of the Poles to fight in 1939 owe more to the structural or the particular? A structural explanation might concentrate upon the fact that Poland was an agrarian society and Czechoslovakia a more industrialized and more urban society, with the result that the aristocracy had greater influence in Poland and the middle classes had greater influence in Czechoslovakia. An explanation centring upon the particular histories of the two countries would point to the long history of wars fought by the Polish kingdom and the fact that the Czechs lost their native aristocracy at the Battle of the White Mountain in the early seventeenth century. Both countries are largely Catholic but why is Catholicism so much more important to Polish than to Czech identity?

At the height of the Cold War, as you saw in Book 4, Unit 26, it was tempting to see twentieth-century history as dominated by a great battle of ideologies and to consider ideology as a major determinant of social change. Great movements, such as socialism, democracy and fascism, seemed to have dictated the nature of societies and to have been the engines of social and economic change. Indeed the end of the Cold War persuaded the American historian Francis Fukuyama that this meant the 'end of history', in the Hegelian sense of history as a great struggle between ideas (*The End of History and the Last Man*, 1992). The twentieth century can indeed be seen to have had a circular history: it ended as it began, with the political and economic systems of liberal-democratic capitalism dominant but much more firmly entrenched in western rather than eastern Europe, while the major threat to stability came from competing nationalisms. Interestingly the league tables for prosperity and per capita productivity are not very different from those of 1900.

Our major concern has been with the effect of the total wars of the first half of the twentieth century upon social change. The central argument is not about whether it was structural forces or wars that promoted change but about how much influence we accord to each. Few would seek to deny economic and technological change first place, while a historian who held that the wars made no difference at all would be foolhardy indeed. It is not just Marxist historians who have emphasized the primacy of long-term structural forces. I would argue that changes in the position of women, especially their greater employment in a whole range of occupations, owes little to the wars and not much to feminists but a great deal to changes in economic, industrial and technological processes: that is, the number of jobs that women could do as well as men increased enormously in this period. There is little doubt that one can make a strong case that, viewed over many decades, the wars can be seen as of minor account compared with long-term structural forces.

As Arthur Marwick has argued: 'Those who conceive of change as essentially caused by structural factors will tend to dismiss the effects of wars as being of minor account compared with longer term structural forces' (Unit 4, p.124). The danger is that the constant promotion of the long term can lead to a failure to ask important questions as to why things happened when they did and in the way they did. Even if we were to accept the primacy of the structural for the long term, the short term may correspond to the lives of generations. World War II may, for instance, have speeded up or slowed down the pace of social change in Britain. A change of pace may not sound very important but it could have had a profound influence on the lives of many people. The usual line is that it speeded things up. Even Angus Calder, who denies that the war made for dramatic social or political change, accepts that its effect 'was not to sweep society on to a new course, but to hasten its progress along the old grooves' (*The People's War 1939–45*, 1971). Actually I think there's quite a good case for the view that it slowed things down. Britain in the late 1930s can be seen as heading for the sort of society that emerged in the 1950s, but World War II deflected it into the sort of society that came about in the late 1940s. This is a subject I shall explore in Unit 30. For the moment, the important point is that I think World War II did make a difference.

A very broad depiction of the development of European society between 1914 and 1955 would stress the continued development of industrialization and urbanization. These developments had largely occurred within free-market systems in western Europe, but had been heavily influenced by state direction in the Soviet Union and were by the 1950s being ushered in by command economies in much of eastern Europe. To what extent were these basic trends affected by war? Such a question has, implicitly, a counterfactual dimension, as it depends on having some idea, if only one extrapolated from pre-war developments, as to what would have happened without the war. One could for instance suggest that without the war industrialization and urbanization would have increased in eastern Europe but that, without the Second World War and the consequent Soviet hegemony in the area, the speed of these developments and their characteristics might have been very different. All those instant towns, with their steelworks and blocks of workers' flats, might never have been built. The rural population would almost certainly have declined numerically in any case but peasant smallholdings rather than collective farms would have continued to characterize much of agriculture.

Many more such questions can be asked. To what extent did the wars increase the strength of the US economy and promote American social and cultural influence in Europe? The increase in motor transport was a massively influential development. Did the wars slow down the growth of car ownership in western Europe, because the manufacture of vehicles for private use was almost everywhere suspended for the duration of the wars? Or did they speed it up, because the production of military vehicles could be readily adapted to production for civilian use in peacetime? Such questions are important and cannot be dismissed by concentrating only on the long term, in which, as John Maynard Keynes put it, 'we are all dead'.

How do we measure change?

The simple answer to this question is to apply both qualitative and quantitative measures to the ten areas of social change outlined by Arthur Marwick in Unit 1, pages 6–8. However, as you have learned by now, it is of little value to attempt to assess the effects of war on social change merely by looking at the state of Europe in 1914 and 1939 and comparing it with that in 1918 or 1945. Mark Roseman's article 'World War II and social change in Germany', printed in the Course Reader (Chapter 14), argues clearly that to answer this sort of question in relation to Germany consideration must be given to the changes carried out by the National Socialist government in its six years of rule before the outbreak of the war. Again, Book 1, Unit 2 demonstrated the importance of understanding the fundamental features of pre-1914 societies, and what changes were already taking place in these societies prior to the First World War. Such an understanding is crucial to any evaluation of the First World War's effects. If you constructed an exercise chart of the changes already taking place in Europe before 1914, as Arthur Marwick suggested in Book 1, Unit 4, you will have a very useful document with which to start your revision. This, together with Book 2, Units 6–13 and Book 4, Units 21–26, should enable you to assess the extent of social change both consequent on the two wars and over the whole period from 1914 to 1955.

3   POLITICS, IDEOLOGY AND SOCIAL CHANGE IN EUROPE 1914–1955

War was an important stimulus to social change in twentieth-century Europe, but it was not the only one. In the Soviet Union from 1917 onwards, and then in eastern Europe from the late 1940s, societies were remade as peasants' smallholdings were collectivized and backward economies forcibly industrialized. The socialist experience in eastern Europe represents the most obvious example of state-directed social change, yet other processes were initiated by politics. The Holocaust, for example, cannot be adequately understood without discussing its origins in the political processes of the Nazi dictatorship. Elsewhere the links between politics – and in particular the political regime – and social change are less obvious, but deserve some consideration.

Our understanding is complicated by the variety of political regimes that existed in Europe between 1914 and 1955. After the end of World War I it seemed that liberal democracy had triumphed across the continent, everywhere but revolutionary Russia. During the 1920s this democratic tide was rolled back, as democracy failed in Italy and in much of eastern Europe. The 1930s saw the consolidation of modern dictatorships of both the right and the left that based their legitimacy on a sense of historical mission. Fascism and National Socialism argued for a new order based on nations united in eternal conflict, whilst Communism promised the liberation of all humanity. After World War II democracy was restored, and prospered in western Europe under the protection of the United States. In the eastern half of the continent it failed and dictatorships were established under Soviet hegemony. I want to suggest ways in which you might think comparatively about the different kinds of regimes and about their social impact.

Bourgeois Europe recast?

In Book 3, Unit 14 John Golby invites you to consider the applicability of the thesis of Charles Maier to interwar western European democracies. Maier argues that what he terms 'bourgeois Europe' – by which he means a Europe in which 'the basic social divisions of a market economy and industrial order' – survived the social turmoil of World War I. Maier argues that violent social upheaval, if not revolution, could be expected as a result of war, and that the 'bourgeois' order was forced to adapt if it were to survive. It had to accommodate the increased bargaining power of organized labour and inherited the mechanisms of direct state intervention in the economy as a result of war. The result was a 'corporatist' system, a definition of which Golby quotes:

> a form of social organization in which the key economic, political and social decisions are made by corporate groups, or these groups and the state jointly. Individuals have influence only through their membership of corporate bodies. These include trade unions, professions, business corporations, political pressure groups and voluntary associations.

> (N. Abercrombie *et al.*, *Penguin Dictionary of Sociology*, 1984, p.55)

Was bourgeois Europe recast in the 1920s? Golby certainly argues that 'some sort of stability' was achieved around the middle of the decade' (Unit 14, p.29). There was certainly greater state intervention in most European states after the war than there had been before 1914, and there was a greater reliance on organized interest groups to determine the scope and nature of this intervention. Golby, quoting from the introduction to the Course Reader, questions Maier's explanation for this, asking 'isn't it equally justifiable to argue that there was a "simple recognition that societies had to be reorganized for peace after five years of total war? Going back to 1914 was impossible"' (Course Reader, p.14).

Maier's argument is based on a picture of European society characterized by antagonistic social classes. His approach leads him to expect that increased labour militancy should have led to greater revolutionary change. His task, therefore, is to explain why it did not. While I would not seek to deny the upsurge of labour militancy across Europe in 1918–20 – indeed, the units are full of evidence of its extent – I would question whether it had the kind of revolutionary potential that Maier assumes. Much labour militancy was motivated, as Unit 14 shows, as much by a desire for greater social justice within existing institutional arrangements as by socialist ideology. In addition, though the strength of socialist parties after World War I was much enhanced, nowhere did they command a majority of the popular vote. What is striking is the strength of non-socialist political forces across Europe, unified often by their desire to protect private property against social revolution.

In thinking about the Maier thesis I would suggest that you try to separate it from the question of the western democracies. In his book Maier compares three cases – those of France, Germany and Italy from the end of World War I up to 1929. One of the countries under consideration, Italy, was not a liberal democracy by 1929. This does not disprove Maier's argument because the state of liberal democracy is not his concern; he is interested in showing us how a 'bourgeois' social order – one based on capitalism and market economics – not democracy, survived the turmoil of war.

Although across Europe non-socialist political forces were supported by majorities, and not all those who supported socialism backed revolution, Europe was racked by considerable social conflict in the immediate post-war years. Stability was achieved by the mid-1920s though this was probably as much the result of an economic upturn as it was of changes in the management of the economy. It would be overstating the case, however, to argue that the political order was recast. Democracy was effectively overthrown by the mid-1920s in Italy and Bulgaria. It never had a chance in Hungary, while Pilsudski seized

there was stability based on the lack of antagonism between social classes.

power in Poland in 1926. The political orders of the countries of 1920s' Europe remained fragile. With the Depression Italian Fascism changed gear; in 1933 German democracy collapsed; while authoritarian regimes swept to power across eastern Europe at the turn of the decade. Though I will turn to the question of democracy in the next subsection, it is sufficient to note here that Maier overstates the degree of stability achieved in the mid-1920s.

Yes, there were trends towards 'corporatism' and greater state intervention in the economy during the interwar years. But such intervention was uneven. In Britain state intervention in the economy was piecemeal, and interwar government preferred to pursue traditional economic policies as much as possible. Italy proclaimed itself to be a corporate state and developed corporatist institutions, yet, as Geoffrey Warner points out in Book 3, Unit 16, this was more about political control than real intervention in the economy. That there were trends towards greater state intervention in the economy is undeniable, and to some extent these trends may have been attributable to the greater bargaining power of organized labour. This can be overstated, however. The nature of industrial capitalism had been changing from 1870 onwards. This emergence of a new model of capitalism brought new forms of state intervention in its wake.

From the 1870s onwards new branches of the European economy were emerging, particularly chemicals and electrical goods, which provided the motor of growth in post-unification Germany. This new pattern of industrialization, which spread across the continent during the interwar years, generated new forms of industrial organization. Such industries were enormously capital-intensive and this generated pressure for considerable industrial concentration. During the interwar years, behind the ideology of market lay concealed state encouragement of greater industrial concentration in order to meet the pressures of this new model of industrial development. In Unit 16 Geoffrey Warner discusses the role of the Fascist state in Italy, which in response to the Depression not only intervened directly in the economy through the state holding company, IRI, but also pushed larger private firms in this direction. According to Warner, the result was that several private companies controlled the overwhelming majority of output in their respective sectors. Such pressures were experienced in economies that were less formally *dirigiste* than Fascist Italy. In Britain the state also encouraged industrial concentration: large firms such as ICI and Unilever in chemicals and Imperial Tobacco were created to stave off competition from the US.

Alongside this process of industrial concentration industry and the state became more interested in the application of 'scientific' techniques in production. In the French context, John Golby mentioned 'Taylorism', which he defined as 'the application of scientific methods in management and the organization of labour' (Unit 14, p.22). This was one innovation that transformed the shop floor; another was the wholesale introduction of mass production, which often meant the reorganization of production around assembly-line methods. Its promotion by both industrialists and the state throughout the interwar years was common to European countries whether they were dictatorships or democracies.

It was this environment that gave rise to a 'corporate bias', or 'corporatist' tendencies in the interwar years rather than a need to accommodate organized labour as such. Economic development necessitated industrial concentration and state intervention; increasingly the state had to take responsibility for economic development within its borders. The liberal market-based ideologies of the nineteenth century no longer seemed appropriate in the age of capital-intensive production. The state increasingly had to deal directly with interest groups rather than individuals, which in turn reshaped political systems across the continent.

The problems of democracy

Mark Mazower writes that:

> the Paris Peace Settlement saw parliamentary democracy enthroned across Europe. A belt of democracies – stretching from the Baltic Sea down through Germany and Poland to the Balkans – was equipped with new constitutions drawn up according to the most up-to-date liberal principles. British scholar James Bryce, in his 1921 classic *Modern Democracies*, talked about 'the universal acceptance of democracy as the normal and natural form of government' ... Yet liberalism's triumph proved short-lived.
>
> (*Dark Continent: Europe's Twentieth Century*, 1998, p.2)

Why democracy failed across much of Europe, and by extension why it survived in a minority of states such as Britain and France, is not only an important question for understanding the interwar years, but also one of crucial contemporary relevance.

Here I want to outline some of the factors that made liberal democracies so fragile and vulnerable during the interwar period. I am not presenting an account that will work in every case, or account for the failure or success of democracy in each country. It is important to recognize the enormously different contexts existing in each state; in the units there is more than ample description of some of the very different cases, ranging from the failure of democracy in Italy and Germany to its survival in France and Britain. Before going any further it is necessary to state exactly what we mean by 'liberal democracy'. A liberal democracy can be defined as a state based upon the participation of the people, yet limited by the rule of law.

nationalities

The first set of problems are those that relate to the territory and population governed by post World War I liberal democracies. In central and eastern Europe nation states were created that claimed authority over territory that was not exclusively populated by members of the nation that claimed leadership in the state. I introduced this problem in Book 2, Unit 13, with my descriptions of the population mixes of Poland, Czechoslovakia and Yugoslavia in 1919, and some of the difficulties this caused. In the case of Czechoslovakia the German population was never fully incorporated into the new democracy; it was refused autonomy by Prague, and continued to have its own separate parties. Tension only became acute in 1935 when the pro-Nazi *Sudetendeutsche Partei* polled most votes among Germans. Yet this did not prove fatal to Czechoslovak democracy – the most successful democracy in interwar eastern Europe. Instead it was the Nazis who destroyed the democratic system in 1938. In Yugoslavia, however, tension between Croats and Serbs, who dominated the government, army and bureaucracy, led to considerable political instability, which in turn led to a *coup d'état* by King Alexander in 1929. Tensions over territory certainly undermined democracy. The political tension in Germany over the borders established at Versailles provided fertile ground for the anti-democratic right, and for critics of the political order during the years of the Weimar Republic. Resentment in post World War I Italy about the territorial awards made to her as a result of participation in war provided the backdrop to the rise of right-wing nationalism in the country, which was a direct precursor to Fascism.

The impact of World War I itself contributed to the fragility of democracy. The disappointment of demobilized ex-servicemen with the conduct of their politicians, and perceptions that they had been betrayed at the conference table fed political discontent, and violence. The economic impact of the war sharpened class tension that had, in turn, been fuelled by the experience of war and by revolution elsewhere. The German Revolution, Italy's *biennio rosso*, and heightened lower-class militancy across the continent created an environment of instability. In Germany government reliance on right-wing paramilitary groups to neutralize the threat of revolution legitimized political violence, in a way that only served to undermine democracy. The use by landowners in central Italy of Fascist thugs, or *squadristi*, against peasant land seizures in 1920 and 1921 helped initiate the meteoric rise of Fascism. The fear of revolution among Europe's middle classes and the apparent incapability of some democracies to defuse open class conflict also contributed to the collapse of democracy.

If the tense years following World War I directly led to the rise of Fascism in Italy and the collapse of peasantist democracy in Bulgaria, this was not the case everywhere. Hyper-inflation in Germany, Austria and Poland in the early 1920s shook democracy but did not destroy it. Middle-class savings were wiped out by the impact of hyper-inflation yet no immediate collapse of the political system occurred. One might speculate as to whether the experience of hyper-inflation undermined democracy in the longer-term. The best case that could be made for this is that of Poland, where the hyper-inflation of 1923 was followed by three years of political instability, which concluded with the effective end of democracy in the country in 1926. What is crucial to us here is that inflation did not initiate its collapse, though it did expose the inability of the state to protect even middle-class incomes from the winds of economic crisis. Furthermore counter-inflationary measures in Austria, Germany and Poland provoked social tension and industrial conflict, as deflation and unemployment stemmed from the states' attempts to stabilize currencies.

By the mid-1920s the democracies that survived the aftermath of war and inflation appeared to have stabilized. Yet in 1929, with the onset of the Great Depression, democracies across the continent were again faced with acute economic crisis. Mass unemployment and a major recession generated severe social tension during the early 1930s, which spilled over into political crisis. Examining the political impact of the Depression, it would seem superficially that the end of German democracy in 1933 with Hitler's rise to power provides the most convincing evidence for the malign influence of economic crisis on fragile democracy. Yet we would be wise to be cautious before making direct links between economic crisis and the collapse of democracy. In the German case, Annika Mombauer and Bernard Waites argue that:

> the connections between Hitler's rise to power and the economic crisis were more indirect than is often assumed. Before the collapse of the industrial economy, major gains were made among the stricken farming communities

of Protestant northern Germany ... the most solidly pro-Nazi sector of the electorate was to be found among Germany's large self-employed labour force, whether in agriculture or handicrafts.

(Book 3, Unit 17, p.9)

Although economic crisis did lead to changes in political systems across the continent these shifts were not all in the same direction. In Britain the impact of the Depression generated a political crisis over the funding of unemployment insurance that led to the collapse of the minority Labour government of Ramsay MacDonald in 1931, a split in the Labour Party, and the formation of a National government. The National government, dominated by the Conservatives, brought political stability throughout the 1930s. In Sweden Depression and mass unemployment resulted not in the end of democracy but in the extension of social citizenship. The Social Democrats under Per Albin Hansson took power in 1932 and pursued Keynesian policies to combat unemployment while introducing welfare measures that anticipated those that would take root in Britain and elsewhere after World War II.

It is undeniable that structural factors undermined democracy in the interwar period. Economic turbulence did not help, but it would be unwise to argue that economics always determined political outcome. The nature of political systems in each state was fundamental in determining whether democracy failed or succeeded. It is often argued that states characterized by fragmented parliaments elected by proportional representation coped less well with political and economic crisis than those where bodies were elected by majoritarian systems, such as Britain's first-past-the-post system. This argument should also be treated with care. As well as states such as Poland, where a democracy based on a multitude of parties and governed by shifting coalitions failed, there were states such as France and Czechoslovakia, where democracy remained in place. Even in Britain it is important to note that the first-past-the-post system failed to guarantee single-party majority government consistently during the 1920s. Both of the interwar Labour governments, in 1923–24 and in 1929–31, were minority governments that depended upon Liberal support for their survival.

What was more fundamental to democracy in interwar Europe seems to have been whether – given the anti-socialist majority present in most European states – there was a party, or parties, capable of representing the aspirations of that majority that were committed to democracy. States such as the Scandinavian ones, where the left could capture power through the ballot-box, were the exception, not the rule. The situation in Britain, where politics in the interwar years was dominated by the Conservative Party, to which most middle-class electors remained loyal, should be contrasted with that of Germany, where the rise in Nazi electoral support was based on the defection of such voters from a fragmented right. The economy and other structural forces provided the backdrop to the fragility of democracy, but it was politics that proved to be fundamental. *in democracies.*

Debating the nature of dictatorship

Trends towards corporatism coupled with the fragility of democracy characterized the interwar years, yet we cannot survey politics in the period without considering the dictatorships. For many observers the dictatorships of mid-twentieth-century Europe represented by Fascist Italy, Nazi Germany and Stalinist Russia represented an entirely novel form of political organization. All three denied liberal principles that demanded the state recognize a formal separation of powers between it and civil society. They ruled instead in the name of an ideology that stressed the role of the state as a transformer of society, even where, as in the case of Nazism, the governing ideology argued that the state was the highest expression of popular will. All had at their disposal instruments of repression that would have been inconceivable fifty years before. Lastly they made use of new technologies to an unprecedented degree. As Book 3, Unit 18 shows, cinema was used as a means of mass communication, as was radio, creating what some have argued were propaganda states.

The elements that mid-twentieth-century dictatorships had in common have led historians and other observers to characterize all these regimes as 'totalitarian'. From the discussion of each of the dictatorships in Book 3, Units 15, 16 and 17 it is clear that this term is no longer accepted unquestioningly by historians – indeed its applicability has been the subject of much controversy. Each of these units interprets the term 'totalitarian' differently and the respective authors have different positions in relation to it. Here I will briefly go through the arguments about the applicability of the term to the three dictatorships discussed.

Chambers Twentieth Century Dictionary defines 'totalitarian' as 'belonging to a form of government that includes control of everything under one authority, and allows no opposition' (see Unit 15, p.46). We might follow that definition to argue that a 'totalitarian' state is one which aims at, or comes close to attaining, control over all social life under one single authority. This definition might be expanded to include several features that were undoubtedly common to all the mid-twentieth-century dictatorships. These might include: a one-party state led by a charismatic dictator; state control over the economy and over all social organizations, permitting only state- or party-run trade unions or youth organizations; the existence of a secret police force to ensure the consent of the population; an ideology legitimizing state control over all aspects of social life.

On a superficial level these arguments seem convincing, but those who argue against applying the term 'totalitarian' to the three dictatorships have some important points to make. The first is that putting an emphasis on the 'totalitarian' characteristics of the regimes draws attention to the similarities between them and away from the differences. This may lead us to confuse means with ends. Stalin's fundamental aim was not 'total control', but the creation of a new socialist society. Hitler aimed to create the *Volksgemeinschaft*. Concentration on police, propaganda and single parties distracts attention from these more fundamental aims. The Soviet Union was a socialist dictatorship that claimed to be realizing a Marxist-Leninist programme that was avowedly revolutionary and internationalist. It sought the 'construction of socialism', a new kind of industrial society: in Beatrice Webb's words 'a new civilization' (see Unit 15, p.33). This 'new civilization' was a direct alternative to capitalist civilization; private ownership of the means of production, even in agriculture, was abolished, market mechanisms were largely eliminated, and work became both a social right and a social obligation. Nazi Germany did not seek the abolition of capitalism as such. It aimed at a new German, and by extension a new European, racial order, based upon a racial hierarchy, with – as Annika Mombauer makes clear in Unit 17 – definite insiders and outsiders. Mussolini was the only dictator under consideration to argue for a 'totalitarian' state, by which he meant one that expressed the will of the unified Italian people. Critics of the term 'totalitarianism' argue that focusing on the ideologies of the dictatorships and the effects of these ideologies on state action and social change tells us far more about the nature of these regimes than does concentrating on their institutional characteristics.

The second criticism that has been made of 'totalitarianism' is that its use leads historians to overstate the extent to which control came from the centre. In the Italian case it is commonly recognized that the degree of control exercised over social organizations by the Fascist state did not approach that contained in any model of 'totalitarianism'. The monarch remained head of state, while the army jealously guarded its independence. Furthermore the Lateran Treaties of 1929 guaranteed not only considerable independence for the Catholic church from the Italian state, but also gave the church the freedom to organize Italian youth, as well as giving them control over compulsory religious education in state schools. Although Mussolini claimed to be creating a 'totalitarian' state, it would be difficult to disagree with Martin Clark's comment that such 'claims were laughable' (*Modern Italy 1871–1995*, 1996, p.247). In the case of Nazi Germany historians have drawn attention to disorganized decision-making in the Nazi state. In Soviet Russia, where debate has centred on the purges, revisionist historians have also called into question the degree to which they were directed by the centre. Robert Thurston in particular portrays Soviet society in the 1930s as characterized by social tension, which provided fertile ground for the explosion of denunciations that shook the country in the late 1930s. These criticisms suggest that those who have followed theories of 'totalitarianism' have been too ready to assume that control was the primary characteristic of the mid-twentieth-century dictatorships, without subjecting their assumptions to critical scrutiny. Historians have shown that many phenomena were more complex than they have been assumed to be and that, in exploring such complexities, the differences rather than the similarities between dictatorships have been revealed.

polycracy

These criticisms suggest that 'totalitarianism' does not necessarily provide the best framework for thinking about either the motivations of the dictators or the outcomes of dictatorship. Theories of 'totalitarianism' do have two advantages that are worthy of mention. The first is that they draw attention to what mid-twentieth-century dictatorships had in common. Secondly, they underline the differences between liberal democracies and dictatorships – which was why such theories were so influential during the years of the Cold War. In using the term, however, it is important to consider whether the differences between dictatorships outweigh their similarities. It is also important to ask whether the term 'dictatorship' is itself strong enough to capture that distinction.

The question of 'totalitarianism' is important in thinking about the relationship between mid-twentieth-century dictatorships and social changes. If a state really did enjoy a degree of power approaching total control, then it could be considered to be a major initiator of social change. We would expect such a state to be able to reshape society in its own image.

The best case that can be made for this is the experience of the Soviet Union. During the first Five Year Plan, between 1928 and 1932, the country made rapid strides towards industrialization, continued during the later 1930s. Industrial output on the eve of World War II in key sectors such as steel, coal and electrical power generation was dramatically greater than in 1928. Collectivization had transformed the agricultural economy by eliminating small-scale peasant agriculture at tremendous human cost. Peasants flooded into the cities during the early 1930s to take jobs in new industrial enterprises. The Soviet Union had been transformed, though whether it became the 'new civilization' outside model industrial centres such as Magnitogorsk, is open to question. Certainly the state directed unprecedented social change during the 1930s in the Soviet Union, yet it is important to remember that not all the social change that occurred happened according to a script pre-written by the Kremlin. Industrial production increased, but not by the amount originally envisaged by the planners. Goods shortages, materials shortages and labour shortages generated economic crisis in the early 1930s which forced plans to be scaled back. Collectivization was bought at the price of famine in the Ukraine and unprecedented violence across the union, yet the industrial organization of agriculture failed to feed the enlarged urban population. The state banned strikes but could not control its new working class, who shifted from job to job in search of better pay. Urban centres were marked by widespread crime and disorder during the 1930s, which even the Stalinist state seemed powerless to stop.

In the cases of Nazi Germany and Fascist Italy the role the dictatorships played in directing long-term social change is even more difficult to pin down. In Italy, it is often argued that the Fascist state did little to reshape longer-term patterns of social change. In Germany the issue of the impact of the Nazi state on society is at best a contentious one. Few would deny that Nazi racism and anti-Semitism, institutionalized during the 1930s in peacetime, prepared the ground for the Holocaust that eliminated large sections of the Jewish population across Germany and central and eastern Europe. Nazi social policy brought a degree of social welfare and the benefits of consumerism to those who were considered full members of Hitler's *Volksgemeinschaft*. It excluded those outside it. It is more debatable whether Nazism left deeper long-term traces on German society. Although it sought to create a new racial order it did little to alter inequalities based on class, while it probably reinforced pre-existing gender roles.

This schematic discussion of the impact of the mid-twentieth-century dictatorships on social changes does not give credence to notions of 'totalitarianism'. It suggests that everywhere the impact of state-directed social change was limited, though not limited in the same way or to the same extent in every state. Above all it suggests a marked difference between the Soviet Union, which was committed to dictatorial socialism, and Nazi Germany and Fascist Italy, where the social impact of dictatorship, at least domestically, was much more limited. This takes us back to our discussion earlier in this section of the ideological differences between the dictatorships. It suggests that differences between the dictatorships were as important, if not more so, than differences between dictatorships and democracies during our period.

The spread of Stalinism in post-war Europe

Fascist Italy and Nazi Germany were defeated in World War II. The prestige and power of the Soviet Union was greatly enhanced, and this new role gave the Soviets the opportunity to export their model of socialism throughout central and eastern Europe. Victory by domestic partisans in Yugoslavia and Albania also created scope for the transformation of those countries along socialist lines. Although the transitions to communist rule differed in different countries, under the pressure of deteriorating superpower relations from 1947, limited pluralism was eliminated and dictatorships were established on the Soviet model. The new rulers of eastern Europe introduced five-year plans designed to fulfil Soviet demands for armaments to fight a new war that Stalin confidently expected would break out between the Soviet Union and the US in the mid-1950s. Collectivization campaigns were introduced, albeit with less severity than those in the Soviet Union.

State-directed change was imposed on the societies of eastern Europe during the early 1950s. Traditional élites were effectively removed from their positions of privilege, individuals of working-class origin were promoted into managerial positions, the police and the state bureaucracy. The countries of the region were industrialized as urban populations increased and those employed in agriculture fell. Prison populations across the region expanded enormously to 1953, as political dissidents mixed with criminals in networks of labour camps.

These new dictatorships rested on weak foundations. In no state except Czechoslovakia had the Communist Party won a democratic mandate in the post-war period. Some countries had not been allowed free elections and some of those that had, such as Hungary, had voted overwhelmingly for the most anti-communist party contesting the elections. The central European states in particular faced the imposition of a Soviet model on societies that were more advanced than Soviet society. These structural factors alone bred political tension. This was combined with the social consequences of Stalinist policies: collectivization reduced many agricultural households to penury; the demands of financing industrialization cut workers' real wages; the disruption to agricultural production and the disorganization of the planned economy resulted in food shortages in the towns.

Eastern Europe's dictatorships faced economic crisis by the time of Stalin's death in 1953. Shortly afterwards it was to turn into political crisis as the regimes sought to undo the damaging legacy of their brief Stalinist experiences. In May 1953 serious political unrest hit Pilsen in Czechoslovakia, followed in June by upheaval in the GDR. As de-Stalinization gathered pace it combined with popular anger to produce spectacular upheaval in Poland and Hungary in 1956. In Hungary Soviet troops were used to restore order after the dictatorship effectively collapsed in October. Yet Soviet troops would not be sufficient to stabilize these regimes. Increasingly they paid greater attention to the living standards of their populations, expanding social welfare and developing a surrogate consumerism across the block. Yet their industrial economies, undermined by endemic inefficiency and low productivity, would become increasingly unable to pay for the standards of living necessary to keep their populations off the streets.

Renewed democracy in western Europe

Between 1947 and 1949 Europe was effectively divided into two opposing camps, a division sealed by the creation of two separate German states on each side of the ideological divide in 1949. With the exception of Francoist Spain and Salazar's Portugal all the states of western Europe could be described as liberal democracies. All excluded communist parties from their governments. France and Italy had mass communist parties, though both had been kicked out of the governing coalitions in 1947. In defeated Germany and Italy catch-all conservative parties, the Christian Democrats in Italy and the CDU/CSU in West Germany, dominated governments from the late 1940s onwards and presided over their countries' reconstructions.

In contrast to the interwar period, democracy, outside Greece, was to prove extraordinarily stable in post-war western Europe. With the peaceful transitions to democracy in Spain and Portugal in the mid-1970s and then with the 'velvet' revolutions in eastern Europe in 1989, the post-war years present a remarkable contrast to those in the middle of the century. The stability achieved presents a real contrast to the dictatorships across the Iron Curtain, which were shaken by political crises in 1953, 1956, 1968 and then in 1980–81. Moments of crisis in the west, such as the events of May 1968 in France, had limited effects on the political system.

Fascism was largely banished from the political stage in 1945 and, apart from periodic upsurges, far right or post-fascist parties were politically marginalized for most of the post-war period. This marginalization contrasts with the strength of catch-all conservative parties across western Europe, which provided a home for a variety of shades of right-wing opinion and were firmly anchored within the democratic camp. Anti-communism provided an ideological cement which bound most shades of right-wing opinion to conservatism and to political democracy.

Furthermore the 1950s, and later the 1960s, were periods of economic boom. Post-war reconstruction supported by the US, underpinned by the economics of the Cold War, resulted in wholesale social transformation. The rise of modern mass consumerism, generalized prosperity and improved social welfare resulted in tangible improvements in the lives of the majority of western Europeans. This economic success undoubtedly underpinned the political success of democracy. Thus was set the political stage on which the Cold War would be fought across the continent.

4 CONTINUITY, STABILITY AND CONVERGENCE IN WESTERN EUROPE c.1905–1955

The world of 1911 seems remote when viewed from the modern age. We look back, over wars and revolutions, to a world of gas light, music hall and hansom cab, which seems vastly different from our own. We should expect these differences to be reflected in the occupational groupings of the labour force, and yet the dominant fact, then and now, is the preponderance of the group of manual workers. The professional class has remained an insignificant proportion of the whole.

(G. Routh, *Occupation and Pay in Great Britain 1906–60*, 1965, p.6)

This passage, from an indispensable statistical study of Britain's occupational structure and income relativities during the period of this course, is a salutary reminder that the more some things changed, the more others remained much the same. British society in 1960 was *measurably* much more like British society in 1910 than in the year 2000. Not only did the great majority of men in 1960 still make their living as manual wage-earners, the world of paid employment remained predominantly male. The female proportion of the labour force was not much greater than it had been in 1911 (33.5 per cent as opposed to 29.5 per cent). The two world wars had had *no* measurable effect on the rate at which women entered paid employment in peacetime: their labour force participation rate in Edwardian Britain was higher than it was between the wars and during the period of post-war reconstruction after 1945. The proportion of women going out to work did not begin to rise until the 1950s. The ratio of women's full-time earnings to men's improved only marginally between the early and the mid-twentieth century. Those arguing for a significant relationship between total war and the socio-economic aspects of gender relations should find Tables 29.1 and 29.2 rather sobering.

Table 29.1   Percentage of females of working age participating in the UK labour force

Year	Females of working age who were 'economically active' (%)
1911	35.32
1921	33.71
1931	34.20
1951	34.73
1961	37.49

1941: ?

where's the war figures??

(Source: A. H. Halsey (ed.) *Trends in British Society since 1900*, 1972, Table 4.4)

Table 29.2 Women's median full-time earnings as a percentage of men's

Year	Women's earnings as a % of men's
1906	50.2
1938	50.5
1960	53.5

(Source: Routh, 1965, p.58)

Equally sobering is the evidence that the wars had no measurable impact on rates of social mobility in Britain. A large-scale sociological enquiry carried out in 1949 found a high degree of self-recruitment of occupations and no consistent trend for manual workers' sons to move into professional and executive occupations (D. Glass (ed.) *Social Mobility in Britain*, 1954). Short-range mobility – from a skilled manual to a supervisory or more generally 'lower-middle-class' position – was quite frequent, but it does not appear to have become significantly more frequent over time. There is, in short, no macro-sociological evidence that British society was more 'open' in 1951 than it was in 1911, despite the common ordeals and massive disruptions of two world wars.

Britain, you may well be thinking, was unique among the European belligerents because it was insulated from the traumas of invasion and defeat, and shielded from the hyper-inflation which twice wiped out personal savings in Germany. The British people never experienced a discontinuity as profound as '*Stunde Null*' (Zero Hour) in May 1945, nor were they presented with an opportunity for a clean break with the past, such as fell to the French and Italian national communities at the Liberation. The British voted in a new government in July 1945, but the French and Italians had to reconstitute their states. In the process, they committed themselves to principles that promised far-reaching social change. The Constitution of the Fourth Republic, for example, 'guaranteed to women in all domains rights equal to those of men'; Article 3 of the new Italian Constitution provided for 'equality without distinction as to sex'. Defeat, and the overthrow of authoritarian regimes, had – *it would seem* – rendered German, French and Italian society much more malleable than British.

I set out in this section to test that proposition by comparing the macro-economic data on the occupational structures and income relativities of Germany (Federal Germany after 1949), France, Italy and Britain in the first half of the twentieth century. Unfortunately, while structural change in the labour forces and women's participation rates can be readily established, it is much more difficult to compare the systems of rewards and economic inequality over time. Genuinely comparative data on the distribution of income and property are frustratingly hard to find. My aim became the more modest one of drawing your attention to strong elements of continuity in capitalist economic growth in western Europe in the twentieth century and to the relative stability of the social formations in this part of the world. (Relative, that is, to the societal upheavals effected in communist states, where agriculture was collectivized and most property in production socialized.)

Some people jib when they read 'capitalist', as if it betrays some ideological or – heaven forbid! – theoretical prejudices on the part of the person using it. But it is, I think, an appropriate word to describe economies in which property is predominantly in private hands and goods, services and production factors are mainly allocated through market mechanisms. It is particularly apt if we are considering how, in such economies, total output has grown faster than population, and so raised average incomes and living standards. Capital accumulation, which enables entrepreneurs to invest in technological innovation, is the basic source of growth and development. My usage is, I hope, value-neutral, though *in itself* it implies a fundamental continuity in economic life. Andrew Shonfield put the point well when he defended the title of his *Modern Capitalism* (1965), a major survey of economic institutions (public and private) and their roles in promoting growth in post-war western Europe and North America:

> I have decided to stick to the old-fashioned capitalist label ... because I believe that our societies continue to possess many characteristics which are inextricably connected with their antecedents in the nineteenth and the first half of the twentieth centuries; the word helps to emphasize the continuity. There are, after all, still large areas of economic activity which are open to private venture capital, and in these areas its success or failure is determined by the familiar ingredients: the amount of liquid funds available, the efficiency with which they are manipulated, the personal initiative of the controllers of this private wealth and the enterprise of competing owners or managers of private capital. Moreover, the prizes for individual success are still large, and they convey on those who win them considerable economic power.
>
> (Shonfield, 1965, p.3)

Economists of Shonfield's generation had grown to maturity during the world economic Depression of the 1930s, and it was with palpable delight that they spent much of their professional lives trying to explain why, after the most catastrophic war in history, capitalism entered a 'golden age'. At the close of your period of study, the recently devastated western European economies were growing more quickly than they had ever done. Table 29.3 puts this economic resurgence into broad historical perspective. In the two decades or so before the outbreak of the First World War, gross domestic product (GDP) in western Europe grew at the compound rate of 2.6 per cent per annum. (It is referred to as 'real' GDP in the table because allowance has been made for monetary inflation.) This was substantially faster than the growth in population, so real GDP per capita increased at 1.7 per cent annually, which was an unprecedentedly high rate. Here lay the economic basis of what, for European élites, was the *belle époque*. When John Maynard Keynes looked back on the pre-1914 world from the perspective of the Versailles Peace Conference, it seemed to him that

> Europe was [then] so organized socially and economically as to secure the maximum accumulation of capital. While there was . some continuous improvement in the daily conditions of the life of the mass of the population, Society was so framed as to throw a great part of the increased income into the control of the class least likely to consume it ... [I]t was precisely the *inequality* of the distribution of wealth which made possible

those vast accumulations of fixed wealth and of capital improvements which distinguished the age from all others.

(Keynes, *The Economic Consequences of the Peace*, 1919, p.18; original emphasis)

The dominating events in the period 1913–50 were the two world wars and the world economic crisis of 1931–33. Their net result was that the western European economies grew slowly on average (on a per capita basis, by 1 per cent annually). As we shall see, this average masks a convulsive contraction in economic activity and output in 1944–46. The western European economies recovered rapidly from this nadir and entered their most sustained period of expansion. In 1950–73, per capita GDP grew at nearly four times the rate achieved in the years 1913–50 and over twice that of the late nineteenth-, early twentieth-century *belle époque*. What distinguished the 'golden age' was the coming of truly mass prosperity: taking 1953 as 100, the index of real wages in 1970 was 239 in Germany, 277 in Italy, 180 in France, and 145 in Britain (H. van der Wee, *Prosperity and Upheaval: The World Economy 1945–1980*, 1987, Table 27).

Table 29.3   Economic growth in western Europe 1890–1973 (average annual growth)

	Real GDP	Population	Real GDP per capita	Real GDP per person-hour
1890–1913	2.6	0.8	1.7	1.6
1913–50	1.4	0.5	1.0	1.9
1950–73	4.6	0.7	3.8	4.7

Countries covered = Austria, Belgium, Denmark, Finland, France, Germany, Netherlands, Norway, Sweden, Switzerland, UK, all adjusted for boundary changes.

(Source: N. Crafts and G. Toniolo (eds) *Economic Growth in Europe since 1945*, 1996, Table 1.1)

From Table 29.4, you will observe that the broad historical periodization of Table 29.3 is reflected in the growth rates of the four largest western European economies, but with significant national deviations. In the early twentieth century, manufacturing and construction accounted for only one-fifth to one-quarter of Italy's national product, which meant that the very rapid industrialization occurring in Turin and elsewhere had only a limited impact on the overall growth rate. You may be surprised to learn that, around 1910, the proportion of national product generated by manufacturing, mining and construction was much the same in Germany, France and Britain (between 40 and 44 per cent). The big difference lay in the diminutive size of British agriculture, which generated only 6 per cent of Britain's national product, compared with 32 per cent in France and 23 per cent in Germany. Per capita growth in these three economies was very similar during the pre-1914 decades but, while Britain sustained the same modest rate of increase up to mid-century, France and Germany experienced violent fluctuations. In the 1950s, British per capita growth was slow by comparison with the other countries, but very respectable in relation to past performance. Much of the divergence was due to the fact that Britain's level of industrial output in the late 1940s was far higher, so there was less opportunity for 'catching up'. There were, for example, 784,000 motor vehicles produced in Britain in 1950 compared with 357,000 in France and 301,000 in Federal Germany. It only became evident around 1957 that there was a more fundamental divergence between the slow-growing British economy and its dynamic European competitors.

Table 29.4   Average annual percentage rates of growth of GDP in France, Italy, Britain and Germany 1870–1959 (per capita in brackets)

	1870–1913	*1913–50*	*1950–59*
France	1.6 (1.4)	0.7 (0.7)	4.6 (3.5)
Italy	1.4 (0.7)	1.3 (0.6)	5.8 (5.3)
Britain	2.2 (1.3)	1.7 (1.3)	2.7 (2.2)
Germany (Federal Germany after 1949)	2.9 (1.8)	1.2 (0.4)	7.8 (6.5)

(Source: van der Wee, 1987, p.50)

A focus on the common process of capitalist growth does not in any way detract from the manifest dissimilarities between the French, British, German and Italian economies for much of the twentieth century. They had different endowments of natural resources: Britain and Germany were rich in coal, France modestly endowed, Italy had none. France had a comparatively favourable ratio of good agricultural land to labour, and so there was not the pressure to migrate experienced in the comparatively barren Italian South. Britain had embarked on the industrialization process much earlier, and when the majority of the labour force was already employed in manufacturing and services. By 1911, fewer than one in eleven workers were in agriculture. In the continental economies, the proportions were three to five times greater: they had large reserves of labour on which industry and construction could draw during the post-war boom without putting upward pressure on wages. At the beginning of the twentieth century, small-scale employment was the norm in all four economies: even in Germany, where industrial concentration was most advanced, 95 per cent of all industrial establishments had ten or fewer employees in 1907 (though they accounted for less than two-fifths of employment). In France and Italy, the small-firm sector proved much more persistent than in Britain and Germany. Establishments employing fewer than ten wage-earners represented 58 per cent of the French industrial workforce in 1906, 34 per cent in 1931 and 25 per cent in 1954.[1] Astonishing though it may seem, there were twice as many industrial enterprises in France in 1970 as there were in the US. Forty-five per cent of employment in Italian manufacturing at this time was in establishments with fewer than fifty workers. Post-war Britain was rather unusual in *not* having an extensive network of small-scale manufacturers, as Table 29.5 makes clear. Other persistent dissimilarities will be mentioned in the course of the discussion.

---

[1] It is worth noting, however, that the French censuses defined an '*établissement industriel*' as any place of work *producing* a good: it could be a baker's (but not a butcher's) or an armaments factory.

Table 29.5   Small-scale manufacturing firms in 1963

	Number of firms employing fewer than ten persons	Proportion of total manufacturing employment (%)
Italy	245,000	18.5
France	186,000	10.8
Germany	157,000	6.2
Britain	27,000	2.1

Exercise   I would like you to use the data in Tables 29.6, 29.7 and 29.8 to make some basic comparisons of change over time. Table 29.6 shows the growth in GDP per head in selected years in our four countries; to facilitate comparison the totals are expressed in 1985 US$. There are considerable technical difficulties in compiling such data, particularly for the years before 1950 when national accounting methods were not standardized, and the data should be treated with caution.

Table 29.7 gives you an indication of the collapse of GDP in western Europe at the end of the Second World War. Table 29.8 shows the distribution of employment between industrial groups (which are defined by output). The industrial distribution of labour is not the same as the occupational structure: many 'white-collar' clerical workers were employed in mining, manufacturing and construction and a few manual workers worked in commerce and finance. But examining employment in the major industrial groups gives a better sense of the changing pattern of demand for labour than looking at the occupational structure. I would now like you to calculate the ratios of French, German and Italian GDP to British GDP at the selected dates using the information given in Table 29.6. (All you need do is set British GDP at 100. Then divide, say, French GDP in 1913 by British GDP in 1913 (i.e. 2,734 divided by 4,024) and multiply by 100. The result to the nearest round number is 68.) What do the changing ratios tell us about the differing rates of economic growth in the four countries? Bearing in mind the information in Table 29.7, what do you think is the great paradox – or conundrum – of post-war growth in western Europe? What long-term changes in the distribution of employment between industrial groups can you identify? What type of employment grew most quickly in the 1950s and 1960s? Would you say these economies were becoming more or less similar? ■

Table 29.6   Levels of GDP per head of population in France, Britain, Italy and Germany (expressed in 1985 US$)

	1913	1938	1950	1973
France	2,734	3,539	4,149	10,323
Britain	4,024	4,786	5,651	10,063
Italy	2,087	2,595	2,819	8,568
Germany	2,606	4,101	3,339	10,110

(Source: Angus Maddison, *Dynamic Forces in Capitalist Development*, 1991, Table 1.1, except for 1938 data, which have been interpolated from M. Harrison (ed.) *The Economics of World War II*, 1998, Table 1.1)

Table 29.7   Pre-war year when GDP was the same as in 1945

France	1891
Germany	1908
Italy	1909
Britain	never

(Source: Crafts and Toniolo, 1996, Table 1.2)

Table 29.8   Distribution of the labour force by major industrial groups in Germany, France, Italy and Britain, selected years (%)

	Agriculture, forestry and fishing	Mining, manufacturing, construction	Commerce, finance, etc.	Transport and communications	Other services
Germany 1907	36.6	40.9	6.7	3.8	11.0
Germany 1950	18.7	44.9	10.3	5.5	20.5
Germany 1970	7.5	47.9	19.8	5.4	19.4
France 1911	41.0	33.1	9.8	3.4	12.7
France 1954	27.0	36.3	11.1	5.3	20.3
France 1975	10.0	38.4	21.7	6.0	23.9
Italy 1911	55.4	26.6	5.6	3.3	9.0
Italy 1951	42.2	32.1	7.7	4.0	14.0
Italy 1971	16.4	42.2	14.2	5.0	22.3
Britain 1911	8.7	51.6	4.9	8.8	25.9
Britain 1951	5.0	49.1	14.0	7.7	24.2
Britain 1971	2.9	37.9	23.6	9.0	26.5

(Source: Calculated from B. R. Mitchell, *International Historical Statistics: Europe, 1750–1993*, 1998, Table B1)

Specimen answer   The GDP ratios you calculated should be as shown below:

	1913	*1938*	*1950*	*1973*
France	68	74	73	103
Britain	100	100	100	100
Italy	52	54	50	85
Germany	65	86	59	100.5

The ratios indicate that both Germany and France were 'catching up' with Britain, the wealthiest European society, between 1913 and 1938, although the German rate of increase in total product was distinctly faster than the French over the long term. There seems to have been a faint tendency on Italy's part to narrow the gap, but average income was only about half the British level when war broke out. One explanation of this is to be found in Table 29.8: in 1951, over two-fifths of Italian labour was still employed in agriculture, where productivity was very low. The economic collapse in the final year of the Second World War wiped out a whole generation's economic advance in continental western Europe. In Britain, GDP was greater than it had ever been, but other countries were as poor as they had been at the turn of the century. Paradoxically, though, the countries most adversely affected, Germany and Italy, grew most rapidly after 1950. France recovered remarkably quickly from the terrible economic dislocation of 1944–45 and enjoyed exceptionally smooth growth in the post-war decades. French per capita income overtook the British level in the early 1960s. Given the comparative advantages of the British economy in the late 1940s, its mediocre performance thereafter is a real conundrum. We shall have to consider whether the new social settlement – based on the Beveridge Report and a bipartisan commitment to full employment – was at the root of economic decline. Generally, though, it is evident that a process of *convergence* was at work in the four post-war countries: the poorest, Italy, was 'catching up' with the others and by 1970 the 'spread' of per capita GDP ratios was narrower than it had ever been.

Convergence is also evident in the changing distribution of labour between industrial groups. Italy, France and to a lesser extent Germany experienced a sharp decline in agriculture and some growth in secondary sector employment. But, as you can see, the percentage drop in agricultural employment in France and Italy between the 1950s and the early 1970s was in both countries greater than the percentage increase in employment in mining, manufacturing and construction. This means, of course, that employment in services, or the tertiary sector, was increasing more rapidly than any other type of work – which is typical of modern advanced economies. It is worth noting that employment in commerce and finance was proportionately much the same in Britain, France and Germany by the early 1970s. Britain entered the 'services' phase of development somewhat earlier than the other economies: in peacetime, the tertiary sector had been growing more rapidly than manufacturing since the later nineteenth century, though the two world wars temporarily reversed this trend. Employment in British manufacturing peaked around 1950, but then went into a steady relative decline.

I must, nonetheless, emphasize that the growth of industrial *output* was the dynamo of the long post-war boom. The greatest productivity gains were made in manufacturing, principally by learning from American production and managerial practices. By the late 1960s, the proportion of national product generated by manufacturing, mining and construction was quite similar in all four economies: it was 52 per cent in Germany, 48 per cent in France, 46 per cent in Britain and 41 per cent in Italy.

Discussion   There can't be much debate about the *proximate* cause of post-war Britain's mediocre economic performance: as Table 29.9 shows, labour productivity grew at less than half the rate attained in its European competitors. The expansion of British manufacturing ouput was hobbled by a truly dismal productivity record in the 1950s (see Table 29.10). Taking 1950 as 100, the index of industrial production in Germany in 1969 was 404; in Italy, 418; in France, 291; and in Britain, 175.

Table 29.9   Productivity growth in western Europe 1951–1973

	Annual growth of output per person (%)
Italy	5.31
Germany	5.11
France	4.92
UK	2.24

(Source: Crafts and Toniolo, 1996, p.16)

Table 29.10   Growth of manufacturing output and productivity: Germany, France, Italy and the UK 1950–1961 (% per annum)

	Germany	*France*	*Italy*	*UK*
Output	10.1	5.5	8.3	2.8
Productivity	5.3	4.1	5.2	1.4

(Source: W. Carlin, 'West German growth and institutions, 1945–90', 1996, p.457)

But why was productivity growth so sluggish? There are several possible answers to this, but the most provocative was advanced by Corelli Barnett in *The Audit of War* (1986; Bill Purdue refers to this study in Book 4, Unit 22). In brief, Barnett's thesis is that the necessary renovation of Britain's outmoded industrial economy was frustrated by the determination of middle-class social radicals to build a post-war 'New Jerusalem' around a universalist welfare state. Barnett argues that:

> The welfare state would become ... a prior charge on the national income of ever more monstrous size ... finally [accounting for] 40 per cent of all public expenditure, uncontrollably guzzling taxes which might have gone into productive investment and spewing them out again indiscriminately to the poor and prosperous.
>
> (Barnett, 1986, p.241)

The bastard progeny of 'New Jerusalem' was 'a segregated, subliterate, unskilled, unhealthy and institutionalized proletariat hanging on the nipple of state maternalism' (Barnett, 1986, p.304)

Prima facie, there is some substance to Barnett's argument, whatever we may think of his rococo prose. One longer-term effect of the war was to raise public expenditure and taxation to new plateaux: compared with 1938, government outlays in 1951 were about 7.6 per cent higher as a share of GDP, and about 4.8 per cent was accounted for by greater expenditure on the social services. The share of direct taxes in private income from production had doubled, from 11 per cent in 1938 to 22 per cent in 1950. Universal, flat-rate benefits *were* indiscriminate: about a quarter of social security expenditures were received by the middle and wealthy classes in 1949 (C. Bean and N. Crafts, 'British economic growth since 1945: relative economic decline ... and renaissance?', 1996, p.142).

But Barnett's argument would carry greater weight if it could be shown that the welfare state was placing an exceptional burden on the British economy by comparison with its European competitors, particularly Germany. In fact, social security expenditures as a percentage of GDP were consistently higher in Germany throughout the great post-war boom: the lowest figure was 13.6 per cent in 1954, the highest was 18.9 per cent in 1973. In Britain, the lowest figure was 9.5 per cent in 1955 and the highest 14.6 per cent in 1973. Expenditure on social insurance and health was also consistently lower as a percentage of GDP in Britain. British pensions and other benefits were a distinctly less onerous burden on the economy: in 1965, for example, 3.5 per cent of British GDP was spent on pensions; in Germany the figure was 6.3 per cent. (The vastly greater number of German war widows would probably account for this discrepancy; I have not been able to establish the relationship of German benefits to average earnings.) France and Italy also spent relatively more than Britain on social security (data from P. Flora *et al.* (eds) *State, Economy and Society in Western Europe*, vol.1, 1983, p.456). In comparative perspective, the British welfare state – which retained a large discriminatory element in the form of means-tested National Assistance – came cheap. The high and very progressive tax rates imposed in Britain in the early post-war period were quite normal for western Europe because all governments sought to control inflation by soaking up the spending power of the wealthier classes. Once the austerity of the reconstruction years was over, direct taxes in Britain rose somewhat less than average (Bean and Crafts, 1996, p.136). The only truly exceptional institution in the British welfare state was a tax-funded, free at the point of use health service: it has long been recognized as a highly economic way of delivering health care. Otherwise, high spending on welfare was another aspect of the *convergence* of post-war European societies. □

The rise of the corporate economy

I have, so far, discussed economic growth in an abstract fashion, without any reference to the business firms largely responsible for producing goods and services. Here, I will add an institutional dimension to the analysis of economic continuity by briefly considering the 'rise of the corporate economy'. This refers to a tendency within advanced industrial capitalism for the unpredictable market competition between many producers to be overlain by the organized oligopoly of a few giant enterprises. It is a situation with which we are all too familiar: there are only a handful of European volume car producers; fewer still manufacturers of aero-engines and airframes. In 1914, by contrast, there were 155 motor-vehicle producers in France, then Europe's leading manufacturer and the world's biggest exporter of cars. The infant French aeronautical industry boasted twenty-two engine manufacturers and twenty-seven airframe builders in the Paris region. With the exception of mining and metallurgy (in which production units were on average *larger* than in Britain or Germany) the business structure of French industry was like an ant heap. Three hundred bicycle manufacturers employed 80,000 workers (F. Caron, 'Dynamismes et freinages de la croissance industrielle', 1980, p.278). This was not atypical of western European manufacturing at that time: the markets for consumer durables were socially restricted and manufacturers catered for the tastes of middle- and upper-class consumers willing to pay a premium for quality and diversity. In the late 1930s, a new French car cost twice the average worker's annual wage; as late as 1954, only 11 per cent of French townspeople owned a car, and amongst non-car owners, the number with sufficient disposable income to afford one was small (T. Zeldin, *France 1848–1945: Taste and Corruption*, 1980, pp.281, 294).

Beginning in the 1890s, a highly fragmented business structure was slowly consolidated by the emergence of very large enterprises that integrated functions (such as marketing and raw materials processing) hitherto carried on by separate firms. These new giant corporations were usually joint-stock companies, led by salaried entrepreneurs, and with their day-to-day operations conducted by managerial hierarchies that became increasingly differentiated and formalized. The prototype giant firms were the nineteenth-century railway companies: the capital threshold was too high for private partnerships, and railway operations required a devolved but bureaucratic style of management. In Germany, where the evolution of the corporate economy had gone furthest before 1914, giant firms occurred most frequently in the producer goods industries (mining, metallurgy, machine building) and in the new industries of the 'second industrial revolution' (chemicals, electrical goods).[2] Krupp, the armaments manufacturer, had 73,000 employees by 1913; Siemens, a multinational specializing in heavy electrical equipment, had 57,000 workers in its German enterprises, and a further 25,000 in its British and Russian branches. Other giants included the steel producer Thyssen (30,000 workers) and the heavy engineering firm Mannesmann (15,000).

The huge capital requirements of the capital goods sector prompted close links between the giant firms and the leading joint-stock banks, which in turn encouraged the concentration of industrial capitals through mergers and acquisitions. Bankers are professionally more cautious than industrialists and, to protect their investments, the German banks encouraged agreements amongst producers to maintain prices and limit competition. In this they were aided by a decision of the Imperial Supreme Court that made agreements by firms in Germany to restrict competition legally enforceable. (These agreements would have been illegal under American common law and anti-trust legislation enacted after 1890; I mention this because the American philosophy of business regulation was very influential after 1945.) Cartelization was particularly evident in the heavy industries of the Ruhr and this peculiarly German form of organized capitalism was long associated with schemes for an autarkic German-dominated, 'large economic area' (*Grosswirtschaftsraum*). The newer industries of the 'second industrial revolution' were rather more internationalist in outlook, and in them the tendency to industrial concentration was closer to the American pattern of 'trusts'. A mesh of financial trusts began to link the different firms in the organic chemicals industries in 1904, the year in which Hoechst and Casella formed an association (later imitated by BASF and Bayer). The associated firms agreed to pool profits, pay the same level of dividends and allocate part of the capital to a common holding company in order to cope with the high costs of

---

[2] In Britain, by contrast, the majority of the fifty largest companies at that time were in consumer goods: two-fifths in foodstuffs, semi-luxury foods, and drink and tobacco, and up to one-fifth in textiles.

their research programmes and minimize risks to their investments. Agreements were reached to share patents and licenses to manufacture and extended to market sharing and price fixing (A. Milward and B. Saul, *The Development of the Economies of Continental Europe 1850–1914*, 1977, p.52).

If we shift our focus to the Federal Germany of the 1950s, we cannot but be struck by the degree of institutional continuity between the *Wirtschaftswunder* ('economic miracle') and the Wilhelmine period. Eight out of the ten largest industrial enterprises in 1960 were founded between 1860 and 1890 and had been amongst the largest enterprises in 1913. (Some, like Siemens, dated from earlier private partnerships or family businesses but had become joint-stock companies during the second *Reich.*) Although the two biggest combines of the Nazi era, IG Farben and Vereinigte Stahlwerke, were compulsorily broken up after 1945, Germany's corporate structure remained otherwise intact. There had been no nationalizations – unlike in France and Britain – and the public sector was small by western European standards. With the exceptions of the car producers Volkswagen and Daimler Benz, the largest manufacturing enterprises still specialized in capital goods, and were phenomenally successful exporters. Their re-entry into international markets was triggered by the Korean War boom, which generated demand for machine tools and other investment goods, though few of the firms' products were of recent vintage. In 1952–53, four out of five branded exports were sold using trademarks valid worldwide before 1939 (Carlin, 1996, p.465). By 1960, the 100 biggest firms were responsible for nearly 40 per cent of total industrial turnover, and they employed one out of every three workers in industry. The 'weight' of large corporate enterprises within the total economy had grown, very roughly, threefold since the early twentieth century. Siemens, the largest company, had 300,000 employees by 1970. But, contrary to popular impressions, German industry was not particularly concentrated by international standards and the corporate economy had not grown exceptionally rapidly. Comparisons are fraught with difficulty, but if we take a 'giant' enterprise to be one with 40,000 or more workers, there were thirty 'giants' in British manufacturing in 1972 compared with twelve in Germany and twelve in France. By the mid-1970s, the 100 dominant firms accounted for nearly half the total industrial output in Britain (L. Hannah, *The Rise of the Corporate Economy*, 1976).

Not only had the leading German firms weathered the destruction of three political regimes and the multiple crises attendant on defeat and occupation, the men who ran them had proved to be born survivors. Denazification removed some industrial managers, but did little to disturb the continuity in the personnel of Germany's industrial élite. Many who had risen to leading positions in the Nazi economy remained in (or had re-entered) the élite echelon in the 1960s. Indeed, despite total defeat and devastation, the social structure in the western zones proved resilient; there was no upsurge in social mobility, such as occurred in eastern Europe (V. R. Berghahn, *The Americanisation of West German Industry 1945–1973*, 1986, pp.11, 41). Furthermore, the managerial élite brought to the reconstruction of German industry the working practices, techniques and habits of mind that had served so well in the past. Shonfield made the point with characteristic vividness:

> The defeat, division and chaos which Germany suffered in the 1940s did not wipe out the legacy of the past; it only lifted temporarily the pressure of

history. When the Germans began to reconstruct their economy, they built upon the familiar structural foundation and plan, much of it invisible to the naked eye, as if guided by an archaeologist who could pick his way blindfold about some favourite ruin.

(Shonfield, 1965, p.240)

This is not to argue that the outcome of total war made little difference in the long run to the development of the German economy. On the contrary, the political economy in which firms operated was transformed at the insistence of the Americans, and in ways that reflected American traditions of corporate governance. The Roosevelt Administration had made the destruction of the autarkic, cartelized economic 'empires' of Germany and Japan a major war aim, and hoped to create after the war a liberal, competitive multilateral world trading system – a global economic order that Americans would lead, but not dominate. In pursuit of this policy, US occupation officials were instructed to dismantle the German industrial cartels and re-introduce competition into German industry. Despite the fact that the Ruhr heavy industrial area was occupied by Britain, whose Labour government was nationalizing coal (and threatening steel with the same), the option of taking industry into public ownership was not seriously contemplated. Instead, the two colossi of German heavy industry, IG Farben and Vereinigte Stahlwerke, were broken into competitive units that were nevertheless still viable in the international market. The vertical links between the coal and steel producers were severed, as were the horizontal links between firms that had kept prices up. Initially, too, the German banks which had provided the 'middlemen' of the old, uncompetitive organized capitalism were forced to restrict their operations. The biggest were broken into small pieces and, until 1952, the occupying powers enforced the American principle of 'state banking', which confined each bank with all its branches to a single *Land*. But it proved impossible to prevent the 'reconcentration' of financial power: the investment departments of the big three banks re-established links with large-scale industry which went back, in some cases, to the Franco-Prussian war. The law was changed to suit the facts in 1957.

What spurred on this drive to restore business competition in the 'bizone' (the Anglo-American zone of occupation) was the Americans' recognition, by early 1947, that German economic recovery would be the flywheel of economic reconstruction in Europe as a whole and the worsening tensions of the Cold War. The US saw successful private enterprise economies as the most effective response to the threat of communism (Berghahn, 1986, pp.84–110). Key officials in the State Department, the European Co-operation Administration (ECA) and other agencies advocated 'the politics of productivity' as the long-term solution to Europe's political and international instability: attaining the productivity levels of American industry would, they believe, lead to high-wage, mass-consumption economies in which class antagonisms were muted. Under the auspices of the ECA, European businessmen, engineers and workers toured America's manufacturing plants in order to study the secrets of her prosperity. This strategy to deal with domestic strife within European economies dovetailed with strong support for their closer integration because enlarging the market would stimulate competition, and so raise productivity. As one British Treasury official drily commented: 'The Americans want an integrated Europe looking like the United States of America – "God's own country"' (quoted in M. J. Hogan, *The Marshall Plan: America, Britain and the Reconstruction of Western Europe 1947–1952*, 1987, p.427).

The American model of government greatly influenced both the 1949 Federal Constitution and the political culture of the Federal Republic, which was to have profound implications for the organization of the West German economy. The Constitution made it extremely difficult for central government to play a directive role in economic affairs. Although West Germany was a highly taxed society, the *Länder*, not the Federal Government, were the chief taxing authorities (a situation which paralleled that in the US). Since there was no unified fiscal control at the centre, there was little scope for the type of macro-economic management attempted in Britain. The central government's room for manoeuvre was further restricted by a legal limitation on its borrowing powers. In this new political environment the long-serving Minister of Economics, Ludwig Erhard, championed 'a social market economy' that sought to combine economic liberalism with social responsibility and a harmonious pattern of industrial relations. Nearly all leading industrialists were committed to this concept of the social order by 1960. Erhard had introduced a sweeping liberalization programme to accompany the currency reform of mid-1948 by scrapping most price controls and quantitative controls over the allocation of resources. This left no space within the German political economy for the indicative national planning that had been initiated in France (where the state retained a battery of controls over prices and private investment right up to the 1960s). Both politicians and businessmen evinced a marked antipathy for 'top-down' economic planning, as well the characteristic neo-liberal preference for monetary stability over full employment.

Conclusions

This section begs the counterfactual question: what would have happened had the European peace continued in the fifty years after July 1914? For political historians, answers to that question are entertaining but fruitless speculations: the politics of the European states were too open-ended and indeterminate to allow for the disciplined construction of alternative pasts. Wilhelmine Germany might well have evolved into a constitutional monarchy; the Tsarist and Habsburg empires could have survived by adapting their institutions; Home Rule could have succeeded in Ireland. Politically, many scenarios are quite plausible. But the economies of Europe, particularly those with large industrial sectors and modern infrastructures, were more stable and predictable systems than the polities. Industrialized economies are, of course, subject to cyclical fluctuation, recession and even severe depression, but they are sufficiently predictable for governments and other agencies to put considerable resources into forecasting their growth and development. There is not much dispute about the fundamental factors in economic expansion: the supply of labour, capital and physical resources; the skills embodied in the labour force; technological innovation. If economic historians are in a position to quantify accurately the various growth factors, then they can construct counterfactual 'histories' which are immensely useful in explaining the change that did actually take place. The classic instance of this is a study by Robert Fogel (*Railroads and American Economic Growth*, 1964) of what the American economy would have looked like in 1890 had the railroads not been introduced. Nobody, to my knowledge, has undertaken the immense labour of constructing a counterfactual model of the European economies in 1960 had the two wars not occurred, but there is one work that throws some light on the question. In 1972, three economists published an econometric study that situated French post-war growth in the long-term development of the economy (J. J. Carre *et al.*, *French Economic Growth*, 1975). The statistical series for the output of different sectors demonstrated that France had enjoyed a phase of rapid growth between the 1890s and the late 1920s. By extrapolating this trend of growth until the 1960s, Carre and his colleagues arrived at a counterfactual total output very similar to the one actually achieved. Moreover, the rapidly expanding industries of the late 1940s and 1950s – chemicals, rubber, automobile engineering, electro-metallurgy, hydro-electricity – were precisely those in which France had made swift technological progress before 1929.

Would a similar study of post-war growth in Federal Germany arrive at a similar conclusion? I am scarcely qualified to answer but, ostensibly, no. It may be that an extrapolation of trends in the German economy up to 1914 would produce a counterfactual total output close to that of the 1960s, but not if we took the trend up to the 1920s. German economic recovery in the 1920s was weak and faltering by comparison with France and other parts of the industrial world. The period of great instability and inflationary pressure up to 1924 was not followed by rapid growth: in 1928–29, the index of industrial production was only 14 per cent above the pre-war level. World industrial production (which was dominated by the US) was more than 40 per cent above pre-war level. The weakness of the Weimar reconstruction as compared with that of the Federal Republic was reflected across all dimensions: the share of GDP devoted to investment during the Weimar Republic was historically low and productivity growth was slow. Why the Federal Republic succeeded in creating the conditions for rapid, long-term growth, whereas the Weimar Republic did not, is an intriguing problem for historians. One part of the answer must be that the international context was so different. Federal Germany, like Italy, was incorporated in the late 1940s into a novel historical entity: a western Europe under American political and economic leadership. For the first time in its own history, the US was prepared to enter an alliance in peacetime (the North Atlantic Treaty) and devoted considerable national resources to aiding the economic reconstruction of Britain, France, Germany and Italy. In Germany's case, Marshall Aid counterpart funds financed over 40 per cent of investment in coal in 1949–50, 20 per cent in electricity in 1949–51 and 15 per cent in iron and steel in 1949–51. It had proved impossible to restart these basic industries through private investment and market mechanisms; American aid provided essential 'pump-priming'. In the longer term, the support the US gave to the lowering of national economic barriers, the revival of multilateral trade and European economic integration greatly influenced growth and development in the 'golden age'. This is, perhaps, *the* key difference made by the two world wars: they led to the New World creating a political umbrella under which capitalist growth and development could continue in the Old.

References

Abercrombie, N. *et al.* (1984) *Penguin Dictionary of Sociology*, Penguin.

Barnett, C. (1986) *The Audit of War: The Illusion and Reality of Britain as a Great Nation*, Macmillan.

Bean, C. and Crafts, N. (1996) 'British economic growth since 1945: relative economic decline ... and renaissance?' in N. Crafts and G. Toniolo (eds) *Economic Growth in Europe since 1995*, Cambridge University Press.

Berghahn, V. R. (1986) *The Americanisation of West German Industry 1945–1973*, Berg.

Calder, A. (1971) *The People's War 1939–45*, Granada.

Cannadine, D. (1987) 'British history: past, present and future', *Past and Present*, no.116, pp.168–91.

Carlin, W. (1996) 'West German growth and institutions, 1945–90', in N. Crafts and G. Toniolo (eds) *Economic Growth in Europe since 1995*, Cambridge University Press.

Caron, F. (1980) 'Dynamismes et freinages de la croissance industrielle', in F. Braudel and E. Labrousse (eds) *Histoire economique et sociale de la France*, vol.IV, parts 1–2/1880–1950, Presses Universitaires de France.

Carre, J. J., Dubois, P. and Malinvaud, E. (1975) *French Economic Growth*, Stanford University Press.

Clark, M. (1996) *Modern Italy 1871–1995*, Longman.

Crafts, N. and Toniolo, G. (eds) (1996) *Economic Growth in Europe since 1945*, Cambridge University Press.

Flora, P. *et al.* (eds) (1983) *State, Economy and Society in Western Europe*, vol.1, *The Growth of Welfare States*, Macmillan.

Fogel, R. W. (1964) *Railroads and American Economic Growth*, Johns Hopkins University Press.

Fukuyama, F. (1992) *The End of History and the Last Man*, Hamish Hamilton.

Glass, D. (ed.) (1954) *Social Mobility in Britain*, Routledge.

Halsey, A. H. (ed.) (1972) *Trends in British Society since 1900*, Macmillan.

Hannah, L. (1976) *The Rise of the Corporate Economy*, Methuen.

Harrison, M. (ed.) (1998) *The Economics of World War II*, Cambridge University Press.

Hogan, M. J. (1987) *The Marshall Plan: America, Britain and the Reconstruction of Western Europe 1947–1952*, Cambridge University Press.

Keynes, J. M. (1919) *The Economic Consequences of the Peace*, Macmillan.

Mackinder, H. (1904) 'The geographical pivot of history', *Geographical Journal*.

Maddison, A. (1991) *Dynamic Forces in Capitalist Development: A Long-Run Comparative View*, Oxford University Press.

Mayer, A. J. (1981) *The Persistence of the Old Regime: Europe to the Great War*, Pantheon.

Mazower, M. (1998) *Dark Continent: Europe's Twentieth Century*, Allen Lane.

Milward, A. and Saul, B. (1977) *The Development of the Economies of Continental Europe 1850–1914*, Allen and Unwin.

Mitchell, B. R. (1998) *International Historical Statistics: Europe, 1750–1993*, 4th edn, Macmillan.

Overy, R. J. (1995) *Why the Allies Won*, Jonathan Cape.

Pipes, R. (1994) *Russia Under the Bolshevik Regime 1919–24*, Harvill.

Routh, G. (1965) *Occupation and Pay in Great Britain 1906–60*, Cambridge University Press.

Shonfield, A. (1965) *Modern Capitalism*, Oxford University Press.

Wee, H. van der (1987) *Prosperity and Upheaval: The World Economy 1945–1980*, Penguin.

Zeldin, T. (1980) *France 1848–1945: Taste and Corruption*, Oxford University Press.

Unit 30 THE IMPACT OF TOTAL WAR

CLIVE EMSLEY, ARTHUR MARWICK AND BILL PURDUE

(Sections 1 and 4 by Clive Emsley; sections 2, 5 and 6 by Arthur Marwick; section 3 by Bill Purdue)

Open University students of this unit will need to refer to:

Set book: J. M. Roberts, *Europe 1880–1945*, Longman, 2001

Primary Sources 2: Interwar and World War II, eds Arthur Marwick and Wendy Simpson, Open University, 2001

Course Reader: *Total War and Historical Change: Europe 1914–1955*, eds Clive Emsley, Arthur Marwick and Wendy Simpson, Open University Press, 2000

1   WAR AND REVOLUTION

In discussing, in Book 2, Units 11–13, the upheavals which affected the Central Powers and Russia at the close of World War I, we took as one of our starting points Hannah Arendt's 'little noticed but quite noteworthy fact' that, since the end of World War I, 'we almost automatically expect that no government, and no state or form of government, will be strong enough to survive a defeat in war' (Hannah Arendt, *On Revolution*, 1963, p.15). This, of course, does not mean that defeat in war automatically leads to a revolution, except in the very broadest sense that the violent overthrow of a government or state might be defined as a 'revolution'. The experience of Turkey especially, and this was touched on only very briefly, warns us about making the equation too simple and simplistic: Mustafa Kemal did not carry through his revolution until some time after defeat in World War I, and his successful revolution went hand in hand with a successful war against the Greeks.

Exercise   Defeat in World War I might be said to have led, or to have contributed, to a series of political events and processes that might be understood as revolutions in Austria-Hungary, Germany, Russia and Turkey. Each of these empires witnessed the violent overthrow of the old, existing order, mass participation in politics, and struggles between competing power blocs ending with the creation of a new state and government system. Without wishing to imply that this *should* have happened to the major powers that were defeated during World War II, can you identify any elements militating against similar revolutions occurring between 1940 and 1945? ■

Specimen answer and discussion   In the case of the French Third Republic in 1940, defeat was so rapid there was little opportunity for the kind of collapse of morale and the build-up of internal pressures of the kind that affected Germany and Austria-Hungary during World War I. You might want to argue that neither the government of Fascist Italy nor that of Nazi Germany collapsed internally, that neither lost their nerve in the face of revolutionary threat, thus denying the opportunity firstly for crowds to take to the streets, and secondly for competing power blocs to emerge and struggle for mastery. At first glance there might appear to be some mileage in such an argument. However, Fascist Italy was beginning to disintegrate from early in 1943, with collapsing morale and massive strikes in the northern industrial cities, both of which were brought about by wartime shortages and Allied bombing. 'Northern Italy', argues Martin Clark, 'was one of the few places where mass aerial bombardment proved effective in the Second World War. It disrupted production, it shattered morale, and it forced thousands of people to flee from the cities' (Martin Clark, *Modern Italy 1871–1982*, 1984, p.289). In contrast, however, in spite of the disorganization of much of the Nazi administration, of food supplies and welfare provision, the Nazi authorities remained prepared, and more importantly able, to deal ferociously with bread riots in Berlin even in the last days of the war.

You might seek to argue that both Fascist Italy and Nazi Germany were authoritarian and brutal police states and that, in consequence, even up until the end, their populations were in awe and fear of the regime. I think that such an argument is less valid in explaining why there was no revolution, remembering that, until their respective revolutions, the imperial regimes of Germany and Russia employed their police fairly efficiently and often brutally against opposition. It was a palace *coup* that brought Mussolini down in the summer of 1943, and there were unsuccessful *coup* attempts against Hitler, notably the July 1944 bomb plot. These conspiracies developed in spite of the police state apparatus; so too did the food riots in the dying weeks of Nazi Germany. In Imperial Germany and Imperial Russia it was the internal collapse of the old regimes, coinciding with other problems – military defeat, food shortages, and so on – which brought revolutionary crowds successfully on to the streets and gave politicians, hitherto excluded from power, their opportunities.

What appears to me to be significantly different in World War II was that defeated major powers had large and victorious enemy armies on their territory, and virtually, if not actually, in their capitals, at the time of their defeat and surrender. Such armies – from the Germans in Paris in 1940 to the Allies in Berlin in 1945 – were unlikely to stand idly by and watch a violent and revolutionary struggle for power. Winston Churchill, you will recall from Book 4, Unit 20 (p.31), was vehemently opposed to the abolition of the Italian monarchy early in 1944 when it was proposed by the radical anti-fascist resistance committees, and later, at the end of the year, he authorized the use of British troops against the anti-monarchist rising by ELAS in Greece. Churchill was not alone in his concerns about elements of the resistance movements. The activities and the publicized programmes of the partisans in northern Italy caused anxiety among many liberal and conservative politicians, both Italian and Allied. Cardinal Schuster of Milan spoke for many when he urged the Allies to make a separate peace with the Germans in northern Italy so as to forestall a partisan uprising leading to a revolution.

To the extent that they participated in actions against the wartime governments and were forums for planning their country's future, resistance groups during World War II in general might be said to have been 'revolutionary'. But resistance groups were composed of varieties of political groupings often hostile to each other. In France, for example, while the *Front National* covered the whole country and was increasingly dominated by communists after June 1941, there were also conservative groups like the *Organisation Civile et Militaire* in the north and the Catholic *Témoinage Chrétien* in the south, and *Libération-Sud* was established in the Vichy Zone specifically to unite communists, socialists and Catholic trade unionists against the policies of Pétain's government. Divisions between resistance groups were seen at their most marked in Yugoslavia, where Tito's communist Partisans and Mihailovich's *chetniks* fought each other as well as Germans, Italians and Yugoslav fascists. Tito's Partisans were able to carry out a communist revolution in Yugoslavia at the end of the war; but communist 'revolutions' elsewhere in eastern Europe in the aftermath of World War II were not similarly the achievement of wartime resistance groups. A myth developed, especially among the communists of France and Italy, that a 'revolutionary situation' was theirs for the taking in 1945; even if the Allied victors had permitted revolutions, this myth conveniently ignores the directions given to the communist resisters by their party leaders (themselves following directions from Moscow) to lay down their arms and co-operate with the newly established central governments. □

One of the issues that has recurred throughout this course is the extent to which war has generated aspirations for change. In the conclusion to Book 2, Units 11–13 questions were raised about the extent to which war might have been a radicalizing experience for the soldiers and sailors involved. The evidence appears to suggest that those men most troublesome, and most susceptible to revolutionary propaganda, were those who had little or nothing to do apart from the boring routine of military life in garrisons away from the front line, or in the cramped conditions of warships which scarcely put to sea, let alone saw action. A similar situation of inaction led to the creation of the Cairo Parliament by British servicemen serving in Egypt in 1944. The 'parliament' was scarcely revolutionary: its debates generally focused on those topics which were to become part of the Labour government's programme following the 1945 election; but it greatly worried the military authorities who eventually suppressed it.

Political commissars had been appointed in the Red Army from its beginning to ensure the political loyalty of the troops and to exercise Communist Party authority over the officers. The ideological elements of World War II led to political education in varying degrees in the armies of most of the major combatants. The Nazi Party had set out from the time it seized power to indoctrinate the German military; the process was stepped up on the outbreak of war using radio, film, written propaganda and the spoken word. But during the crisis of the first winter on the eastern front, the army commanders themselves concluded that there had to be an increase in the indoctrination of soldiers to prevent them breaking under the strain. This led to the creation of educational officers in the intelligence units of frontline formations. In the winter of 1943 'National Socialist Leadership Officers' were appointed to all military staffs down to divisional level. In his study of the German army on the eastern front, Omer Bartov concludes that the political and ideological indoctrination of the troops was very successful (*The Eastern Front 1941–1945: German Troops and the Barbarisation of Warfare*, 1985).

In June 1941 the British army established the Army Bureau of Current Affairs (ABCA), which prepared two regular bulletins in alternate weeks, one on the latest military events, the other on current affairs. These bulletins were designed to provide the basis for compulsory weekly discussions at platoon level. The intentions behind the scheme were the raising of morale, the improvement of relations between officers and men, and education for education's sake; but there were many critics who feared the effects of encouraging the army to discuss politics. Not the least of these critics was Churchill, who demanded to know of the Secretary of War in October 1941: 'Will not such discussions only provide opportunities for the professional grouser and the agitator with the glib tongue?' One year later, he suggested to the same minister: 'I hope you will wind up this business [the ABCA] as quickly and as decently as possible, and set the persons concerned to useful work' (quoted in Paul Addison, *The Road to 1945: British Politics and the Second World War*, 1975, pp.148 and 151). Of course, there was a world of difference between the organizers of the ABCA and of the Cairo Parliament, but the concerns about them are both illuminating and significant.

Disaffected soldiers, sailors and policemen, crowds angry about war-induced privations, governments that had lost their nerve – these are all significant ingredients of the revolutions you have studied in the course. But perhaps what all these point to as regards the interrelation between war and revolution in twentieth-century Europe is the way that total war has tested regimes to the utmost. The unconditional surrender demanded by the combatants in such war has meant that defeated regimes were bound to be swept away, leaving a governmental vacuum; but the pressures of such war have also led to some regimes collapsing from within even before total military defeat and unconditional surrender. In both cases there has been political change, but it is in the latter instance that the change is most obviously revolutionary. The men with the revolutionary ideologies have played little part in bringing down the old regimes; it is their own political acumen, their ruthlessness, their luck, and sometimes the support of a major external power, which has enabled a few of such revolutionaries to seize power and hold on to it.

2   THE DEBATE OVER THE SOCIAL CONSEQUENCES OF WORLD WAR I

During the last years of the twentieth century a couple of books by Joanna Bourke attracted a good deal of attention. Their very titles, *Dismembering the Male: Men's Bodies, Britain and the Great War* (1996) and *An Intimate History of Killing: Face-to-Face Killing in Twentieth-Century Warfare* (1999), indicated that fresh, perhaps even slightly shocking, approaches were being taken to aspects of the First World War (and also the Second World War). The first book fitted in with what has become something of a fashion among writers (particularly feminist ones) favouring a theoretical approach to historical and social topics, focusing on 'the body' (remember my opening remarks in Book 1, Unit 3, and my comments on 'the politics of the body' in Book 2, Units 7–10, pp.158–61). The second book, very properly, brought our attention back to the fundamental fact that: 'The characteristic act of men at war is not dying, it is killing' (Bourke, *An Intimate History of Killing*, 1999, p.1). Naturally, certain sentences in the first book please me greatly:

> Systematic analysis about the impact of war was first undertaken by Arthur Marwick, and the resilience of the debate is due in part to his persuasive contention that wartime experiences are crucial if historians are to understand British society and culture between 1918 and 1939.
>
> (Bourke, *Dismembering the Male*, 1996, p.16)

As is apparent from the title, the central topic of this book is the horrific way in which soldiers were injured and maimed in this war, but Bourke also suggests that the general debate over the social consequences of the war has focused on four topics (these collapse and condense the ten topics I have laid out from time to time throughout this course – and which – as Bourke's are too, are relevant to all the European countries, not just Britain). The first, according to Bourke, is the effect of war on population trends and social policy. The second is how war affected social cohesion, political values and relationships between government and populace. The third is the impact of war on women: here Bourke comments that 'Arthur Marwick also contributes to this debate, observing that the war encouraged divorce and "spread promiscuity upwards and birth-control downwards'" – again I'm grateful for the mention, though obviously I've said rather more than that. Even more pleasing for me, actually, is Bourke's identification of the fourth topic as war's effects on 'cultural ideas and discourse'. I take this comment as validating everything we have in the course about war's effects on philosophical thinking, literature, the arts, film, radio, etc. Then Bourke makes a point which we have stressed throughout this course, and which you should have burnt into your brain as you go into the examination:

> Identifying changes as accompanying or following war does not necessarily mean that they were caused by war.

(Bourke, 1996, p.26)

'Arthur Marwick', she continues, 'goes further, warning his readers against adopting the "middle road" in these debates by ascribing everything to the "accelerating" effect of war. As he correctly reminds us, "this simply side-steps the question of why war might accelerate a pre-existing trend"' (Bourke, 1996, p.26). Personally, I caution everyone (fellow historians as well as students) to be very sparing in the use of metaphor. To talk of war as 'accelerating' or as 'a catalyst' is simply to substitute a banal (and actually thoroughly inaccurate) metaphor for the real work of trying to puzzle out the connection between what happens in war and such changes as do come about. You are in no way required in this course to follow the kind of conceptual framework I have set out in my own writings (war as disruptive cataclysm, war as 'test', war as involving the participation of underprivileged groups, war as psychological cataclysm) but you certainly are expected to think far beyond the simplistic proposition, 'these things happened after the war so they must have been caused by the war'. Book 1 of our course gives you a very clear account of what things were like *before* the war against which you can judge the possible effects of the war.

There have always been historians who have argued against giving the war any special attention as a putative agent of change. Certainly, we should always give proper weight to longer-term forces of change (economic growth, demographic change, technological innovation – including methods of birth control), but I would hazard the statement that there is a trend in historical study towards paying greater attention to the significance of events themselves (wars and revolutions in particular). At the beginning of Book 2, Units 7–10 I quoted French historian Patrick Fridenson as noting that, in contrast with an older generation, French historians were now examining the effects of the First World War very closely. English historian Ross McKibbin, back in 1974 in a book relating to the period of the First World War, *The Evolution of the Labour Party, 1910–1920*, went out of his way to ridicule claims I had made in my still earlier book, *The Deluge: British Society and the First World War* (1965), that British society changed over the war period. Later, however, in *The Ideologies of Class: Social Relations in Britain 1880–1950* (1990), he expressed a change of view: 'In my book *The Evolution of the Labour Party* I certainly underestimated the effects of the First World War' (though he made no reference, or apology, to me!). Most usually it is feminist or left-wing writers who tend to deny any special influence to the war experience. Sandra Holton, we saw in Unit 1, prefers to attribute the winning of votes to the carefully judged policies of the women themselves, particularly those in the peaceful suffragist movement. We also encountered in Unit 1 the argument that the only significant development to emerge out of the First World War was the Russian revolution. This is an argument less likely to be put forward these days when fewer historians see the Russian revolution in itself as a desirable event. You may also want to remind yourself that J. M. Roberts does not attribute any special significance to the war in discussing the main developments and changes in early twentieth-century Europe, and certainly he does not examine the war systematically from this point of view. Instead, in subsequently discussing changes relating to the position of women he does suggest that they were connected to the war, but he does this without giving reasons as to why this should be.

Apart, then, from the position that, compared with longer-term forces, the First World War was not of great significance (and, therefore, did not have any social consequences worth bothering about – the Roberts position), we can distinguish four positions:

 1   The war had immense consequences, but these were almost entirely disastrous.

 2   The war had immense consequences, many disastrous, but also several that were positive (this is my own position).

3   Some historians have seen the war as having positive outcomes for Britain, but, implicitly or explicitly, they view Britain as rather a unique case, insulated from the generally disastrous consequences the war had for the other European countries. I have to confess that my own early ideas about the relationship between war and social change were very much governed by the British experience. I have long since recognized that while, with respect to social reform and increases in real income for the majority of the working class, there were positive changes in Britain, working out the outcomes in the continental European countries is much more difficult, with the destructive effects of war being only too evident.

4   Many recent historians have switched away from the more obvious (though, I would still say, important) issues of gains and losses to other (perhaps more fashionable) questions about the impact of war. I have already referred to the highly original works of Joanna Bourke. Much of the new work has been within what I have termed the 'psychological dimension' of war, or 'war as psychological cataclysm'. Much attention has been focused on the fighting men themselves (as distinct from the home fronts and the putative changes taking place there). There have been specialist studies of mobilization, how it was achieved, the effects it had on the wider society, and of demobilization and its social implications. There have been several studies of how the 'trauma', the sorrow and the suffering were represented, remembered and faced up to, in fiction, in folk myth, in memorials. We do not go into these matters, so there is no need for you to do so either. I mention them here solely with regard to the bigger debate over whether or not the war had substantial social consequences.

One argument that is sometimes made against the idea of the First World War having any great significance is that compared with, say, the Revolutionary and Napoleonic Wars which, off and on, lasted for more than twenty years, the First World War was really very short, just over four years. There could not be, it has been argued, over such a short period, substantial changes in people's lives and attitudes. I'll return to that point a little later.

The war as unmitigated disaster thesis comes through strongly in Holger H. Herwig, *The First World War: Germany and Austria-Hungary 1914–1918* (1997), though I'm not sure that Herwig is completely consistent in his utterances and quotations. He begins with a quotation from a rather ancient book, *The Thirty Years War* by the popular historian C. V. Wedgwood (literary in approach rather than scientific), which, he says, applies equally to the First World War:

> The war solved no problems. Its effects both immediate and indirect, were either negative or disastrous. Morally subversive, economically destructive, socially degrading ... devious in its course, futile in its result, it is the outstanding example in European history of meaningless conflict.
>
> (Herwig, *The First World War*, 1997, p.1)

Immediately after this quotation Herwig states that: 'The First World War remains pivotal to understanding the twentieth century'. Perhaps – reflect on this for yourself – there is no contradiction between a 'meaningless conflict' and one which is 'pivotal'. Anyway, Herwig clearly recognizes the war as having been important (and if it is 'pivotal' that means that it must have had consequences), but, equally, Herwig is insistent that these consequences were disastrous. Although his book is almost entirely a military history, he does make some brief comments on those important topics 'the family' and 'the position of women'. The phrase he uses is that: 'The war rent asunder the traditional German "home"' (Herwig, 1997, p.3). If this is saying what I take it to be saying – that the war had highly disruptive effects on the traditional German family – then this is intriguing, since Richard Wall and Jay Winter, in the introduction to their collection of essays *The Upheaval of War: Family, Work and Welfare in Europe 1914–1918* (1988), argue that the war consolidated the traditional family. Of relevance here too is the point that Richard Bessel, from whose important study *Germany after the First World War* (1993) you have extracts in your Course Reader, pays great attention to the adverse moral effects of the war on, for instance, family life. Here we get an illuminating insight into the complexities of the phrase 'social change': if war has disruptive effects on the traditional family and on conventional morality, that is social change, even if historians such as Herwig and Bessel find this regrettable – remember that change does not have to be what those on the political left used to call 'progressive change'. However, to many commentators – including, obviously, a large number of feminists, but also those, like myself, who believe that the loosening of authoritarian constraints can be beneficial for a majority of human beings – disruption to the traditional family could involve 'progressive' social change. Wall and Winter, in making their point, definitely see it as supporting a general position that the war did not lead to significant social change. It goes further than this, for even Herwig seems to recognize that even in a generally disastrous situation there might be gains for some groups of people. The effects of war can be paradoxical: definitely negative in some areas, but at the same time having positive effects in the same areas. Herwig writes:

> By 1918 there existed in Germany a 'surplus' of 2 million women, mainly widows. Many were impoverished by meagre government pensions and

subsidies that failed to cover the escalating costs of increasingly unavailable food. Still others entered traditional 'male' industries and gained unknown independence.

(1997, p.3)

Exercise   Concealed within these (correctly) gloomy statements, one might be able to detect one, or even two, sets of gains, the more obvious one being contained in the final sentence, the less obvious one in the middle sentence (try to remember my discussion of the Bessel extracts in Book 2, Units 7–10). ∎

Specimen answer   I imagine you would have got the point about women gaining independence
and discussion   which we can link to the general question of the emancipation of women as a result of the war experience. At the human level, of course, that is absolutely no compensation for losing a husband or sons. The less obvious point is that, as a consequence of the destructiveness of war (and also the replacement of the Imperial regime by a Social Democrat one), new pensions and subsidies were introduced. (I hope you remember my extensive statistical table showing the way that in nearly all countries big welfare initiatives were taken in the years after the war.) But then, of course, inflation and food shortages (also largely consequences of the war) made these pensions of dubious value. All of this illustrates a fundamental point I have made that in answering questions about social change there is a very complex piece of addition and subtraction to be made. I think it is perfectly acceptable to conclude that in Germany and Austria and in most central and eastern European countries the consequences of the war were overwhelmingly negative, and in some cases perhaps even disastrous. But a good historian does not simply state that. What good historians have to do (and this includes you in writing your exam answers) is look at all sides of the question, examining the case for there having being 'progressive' social changes, even if in the end coming to the conclusion that the negative or disastrous effects outweighed the positive ones. □

The same kind of contradictory or paradoxical picture emerges in the important book *The War from Within: German Working-Class Women in the First World War* (1997) – originally published in German as *Arbeitsfrauen in der Kriegesgesellschaft, Beruf, Familie und Politik im Ersten Weltkrieg* (1989) by the German woman historian Ute Daniel. One of the welfare developments in Germany during the war was the introduction of Family Aid for the families of serving soldiers.

> As recipients of Family Aid and in the absence of their husbands, many women had control over the family's entire cash income for the first time. This enabled them to see the previous mode of allocation within the family, by which the husband had frequently received the largest share of the money or goods, from another perspective ... The assumption that after such experiences, these women were generally prepared to re-establish the status quo with regard to family income after their husband's return is perhaps the most implausible of all possible developments.

(Daniel, 1997, p.188)

In other words, Daniel is hinting, there was a change in the consciousness or mentality of German working-class women. In my own discussion of the role and status of women during and after the First World War I (Units 7–10), I drew attention to the relatively limited (though, in my view, crucial) nature of the expansion in women's employment in Britain over the war period. If anything, probably because of the greater strength of traditionalist attitudes in Germany, expansion was even more limited in that country. However, as in Britain, there was a great improvement in the *quality* of the jobs open to women during the war.

> Especially for maids, agricultural workers and workers in industries, such as the textile industry, whose production either stagnated or decreased during the war, the war boom represented a chance to move out of occupations that either paid less or involved a greater degree of personal dependence. Here, as with the surge of women into office jobs with the military and war societies, the great number of women who changed employment out of their own initiative supports the premise that those women subjectively perceived the opening of new fields of work as a chance to improve their situation. This premise is also verified by contemporary surveys, where, for example, women employed during the war in 'male positions' in the metal industry asserted that they wanted to keep their new jobs beyond the end of the war. Thus, by broadening the spectrum of jobs open to women, the war did bring, objectively as well as subjectively, a change for the better and, thereby, an opportunity for emancipation.
>
> (Daniel, 1997, p.278)

Daniel's comments suggest that improvements for women were essentially temporary. She has a nice phrase which you might care to note: what women got, she says, was 'an emancipation on loan'. She does, however, bring out a perhaps slightly unexpected way in which the position of women changed: because of the new work they took on they became 'a subject of positive national interest'; their work was now positively valued 'as a patriotic service to the war economy'. Some historians have taken the line that there was a great deal of talk about reform and change during the war, but that talk was really all it was. One has to scrutinize the situation carefully, of course, but sometimes talk – talk about votes for women, for instance, in all countries – can actually make the change more acceptable, more legitimate. Almost incidentally, Daniel brings out a rather shocking detail: women accused of being unfaithful to their soldier husbands were placed in the public stocks. The use of the stocks, of course, was swept away in the Weimar Republic. So the argument that the First World War did bring an end to certain authoritarian, antiquated regimes is not without foundation.

On the whole Roger Chickering, in his book *Imperial Germany and the Great War, 1914–1918* (1998), follows the 'disaster' line, though he rather echoes Herwig in suggesting that some new opportunities were created for women, writing: 'While the attendant dislocations [brought by the war] offered opportunities for some categories of workers, like women, the disruptions were general'. He then sets out what he sees as the disastrous effects of the war for Germany:

> The economic crises that punctuated the brief life of the first German republic were legacies of war. The conflicts that flourished in this climate of crisis were themselves long-standing features of life in Imperial Germany,

which the privations and resentments of war had exacerbated – so much so that the war appeared at times not to have ended on the German home front in 1918.

(Chickering, 1998, p.203)

If there were positive social changes, these were most obvious in Britain and France, in that order. And, as I have said, there are those who, explicitly or implicitly, take Britain to be a rather unique case. Alastair Reid (in 'World War I and the working class in Britain', 1988, and elsewhere) has been prominent in arguing that the participation effect of the war worked very much to the advantage of the British working class. With regard to France, I refer you again to the words of Patrick Fridenson quoted at the beginning of Units 7–10.

The recent, less conventional, studies of the war have stressed its deep psychological, its 'traumatic' impact. The arguments put forward by this school of writers at least serve the function of challenging the views of those who say that since the First World War lasted only four years it cannot have had any lasting consequences: if the war was as 'traumatic' as some writers say, then it would indeed have had lasting consequences. Probably the most renowned of the 'new' approaches to the First World War is that developed, though not pioneered, by Jay Winter. Winter is perhaps a little obsessive (as dedicated academics, perfectly understandably, can become when writing on their own specialization) in insisting that *the* important social topic in regard to the First World War is the way in which people mourned the losses of that war. War deaths, of course, were a cause for personal and communal mourning, but the war also – there is plenty of evidence of this – released among ordinary people aspirations after a better, more peaceful, more just world.

Thus far, I have been drawing attention to a handful of books which as a student of *Total War and Social Change* you would be expected at least to know about, and which you might feel like reading at leisure after the exam. Now I am going to work my way through Units 7–10, drawing attention to points that I think you might want to have in the forefront of your mind as you go into the exam. The Introduction draws attention to some obvious, but perhaps too easily forgotten, points. The first is that the war certainly did not lead either to the perfect socialist state (many would now say, reversing Gerd Hardach and Marc Ferro, that it did indeed lead in one part of Europe to a horribly imperfect socialist state) or to complete equality between the sexes – the implication here is that it is absurd for historians to make judgements according to such idealistic standards. The other obvious point is the enormous destructive cost of the war: it is against this that all estimates of positive change must be set.

Section 1 details the aspirations and the errors of the statesmen at Versailles; but never forget those clauses (some of them quoted in *Primary Sources 1: World War I*) which tell us about the new ideology of democracy, social reform and (up to a point!) equality of the sexes felt to be appropriate to a post-war world. Bill Purdue gives a nicely balanced assessment as to how far the war itself (as against the decisions of politicians) was a governing factor in the post-war settlement.

It is undeniable that the war was responsible for both the sweeping nature of change and for many, but not all, of its specific features. The war was responsible for the disintegration of great states and for the changed balance between victorious but defeated nations. The Versailles Settlement was, obviously, the direct outcome of the war.

(Units 7–10, pp.75–6)

In section 2 Bill Purdue goes on to bring out the complexities within the issue of the war's effects on population, being rather critical of some of the assertions made by Roberts. One important point is that we must always be aware of the population *movements* induced by the war and the settlements, and of the effects, in calculating the populations of the individual countries, of the redrawing of boundaries. With regard to long-term developments, both international and internal, the adverse impact on France is particularly worthy of note. Bill Purdue quotes Paul Gagnon's 'succinct' comment that:

> A quarter of all Frenchmen between the ages of 18 and 30 were dead. Six hundred thousand were disabled in body or mind or both. Counting civilian deaths and those unborn because of war, France lost 3 million people. Only the return of Alsace-Lorraine (1.8 million) and immigration enabled her to return to 40 million by 1930.

(Paul Gagnon, France since 1789, 1972, p.329)

A very important general historical point, insufficiently emphasized in many textbooks, is that before the war the European countries were exporting slices of their population to the Americas and such other overseas territories as Australia. This outflow greatly diminished after the war (a fact which needs to be taken into account in discussing population trends): no doubt this was due to factors other than those generated by the war, but it was in keeping with the spirit of national insularity and isolationism and the raising of barriers between countries which characterized the interwar years (American attitudes are obviously particularly important).

I now come to the section 'Social structure'. If you have the time, this really would be well worth rereading now. Bill Purdue brilliantly illuminates a number of crucial issues. He mentions that both Arno J. Mayer and Charles S. Maier belong in the theoretical, Marxist camp, though Maier would probably describe himself as a Weberian. They contradict each other, of course: 'if an aristocratic *ancien régime* persisted up until 1914 [Mayer's view], then a "bourgeois" Europe could not have been *recast* after the war [Maier's view]' (Units 7–10, p.95). Bill Purdue describes the Mayer–Maier approach (which, in shorthand, I have described as 'theoretical') as 'materialistic, teleological and loosely Marxist' and distinguishes it from the 'more empirical view of class' taken by himself and by myself. Major points made in this section are:

1   The overall class structures in eastern Europe and western Europe are very different from each other.

2   The broad frameworks of class structure were not changed by the war, though some of the aristocracies did suffer quite severely. Blows to the many different groups which make up the middle classes Bill Purdue sees as essentially temporary. There were gains for the working class in Britain, but in other countries the situation is much more problematic. He responds to my point about the growth of 'mass society' and consideration for 'the common man', but there remain slight differences of emphasis between us, which I will refer to again when I come to my own sections. Although in

eastern Europe the war and its aftermath was accompanied by land reform, his conclusion is that the material condition of the peasantry did not really improve.

In the section 'National cohesion', Bill Purdue makes a helpful distinction between 'state nationalism' (where national cohesion was encouraged by the state, as in Britain and France) and 'popular or ethnic nationalism', which made a strong appeal to peoples living in societies where government and governors came from different ethnic backgrounds to the lower orders. And consider this statement very carefully:

nationalism

It can be argued that the war's most fundamental consequence was that national identity became paramount as the basis for the existence of states and that increasingly the basis of national identity was ethnicity.

(Units 7–10, p.107)

Now we come to my section 'Social reform and welfare policies'. You perhaps remember the massive table set out on pp.120–4, showing that there were some social reforms before 1914 but that in the years immediately after the war there was a spate of them. I really think the best thing you can do at this point is turn to that table and ponder it again for half an hour or so. If you are doing a question in the exam on war and social reform you will be expected to provide details of specific legislation from several countries, not just vague generalities.

Most historians, I must admit, have not singled out post-war reforms in quite the way I have done. But the more one reads in the histories of the individual countries, the more one comes across bits of welfare legislation that general textbooks have tended to ignore. You will several times have come across the phrase 'pro-natal social policy' (i.e. a policy intended to encourage births, through family allowances and welfare provision for mothers and children). Speaking of such policies being followed in Germany immediately after the war by the national government, the state governments and the local communities, Daniel says they 'marked a further stage in the development of the modern welfare state' (1997, p.286).

Complexity is also a key theme in the section 'Material conditions'. Vital evidence for this topic is contained in the wages and cost-of-living statistics given in Document II.14 in *Primary Sources 2: Interwar and World War II*. You should look at this now and read my commentary on pp.136ff. of Units 7–10. I explain why there were what I term 'ups and downs' in Germany and why generally, in east and central Europe, and in Italy, material conditions were on the whole aggravated by the war experience. There seems to be agreement between Bill Purdue and myself that material conditions improved in Britain, but we are in slight disagreement over France.

In discussing customs and behaviour (the next section) it is, as with social structure, important to make the distinction between the less-developed eastern countries and the western ones. Here is my broad argument (drawn from Units 7–10, p.144):

In both types of country there are, of course, long-term forces making for change in customs and behaviour, but such forces are more apparent in the advanced countries; within the context of long-term change, the war did indeed have identifiable effects in both sorts of country; limited but important changes, which can be related to the war experience, are apparent in the developed countries, but, given their relative level of backwardness, the really striking shake-up, as it were, comes in the less-developed countries, where the cataclysmic effect of war was felt most strongly.

There is no absolute end to the argument as between the effects of war and the effects of longer-term trends. My argument with regard to the less-developed countries would essentially be that because of the disruptions of war, because of the way individuals were projected into new situations and brought into contact with foreign influences, predominantly peasant societies began to adopt some of the customs of western societies. Now one could immediately argue that there was, in any case, a long-term trend towards urbanization, and that this would have happened at some time anyway. So we come back to the point that when talking about the influence of war we are talking about how things came about at the precise time and in the precise way that they did.

I point out that a discussion of customs and behaviour overlaps with some of the other areas of social change in our list, notably popular culture, the role and status of women, and, with respect to institutions and values, the family. Bearing that in mind, I suggest that there are four relevant topics:

1   sexual attitudes and behaviour, the roles of women, and the nature and status of the family;
2   respect for authority, religious observance, etc.;
3   recreational activities: cinemas, public dance halls, radio, etc.;
4   fashion, dress, etc.

I make the point which could be useful to you in answering a number of different questions, that film is a particularly valuable source material in regard to these topics, and I would suggest that if you feel like a little relief from reading, you might look at your extract from the Marie Stopes film *Married Love*: at the beginning of this discussion I mentioned Joanna Bourke's citation (from my book *The Deluge*) of the phrase about the war spreading contraception downwards and promiscuity upwards.

Let me now just remind you of my thoughts on fashion and dress:

> For women the most obvious change was the advent of the short skirt. Now, once again it is true that fashion was changing, and dress lengths were very slightly shortening in the period after 1905 (associated particularly with the French designer Paul Poiret). Nonetheless both shortage of materials and the need for freedom of movement among women engaged in war work, were important developments during the war. I believe also that post-war fashion can be seen very much as representing the desire to make a break from the bad old restrictive stuffy world, and to put a particular emphasis on youth as the only hope for the future.
>
> For men there was a move towards informality (though, as with birth control, this is not to be exaggerated).

(Units 7–10, p.148)

The question of whether or not the war affected the position, attitudes, etc., of women is obviously a central one. I am going to reprint here (with some additional footnotes as a result of suggestions from Clive Emsley) the very valuable table which I compiled for you: consider it carefully.

Votes for women (and men!)

Dates of introduction of votes for women, and of universal male suffrage.

	Pre-war (over 21 unless otherwise stated)		War and post-war (over 21 unless otherwise stated)	
	Women	Men	Women	Men
Finland	1906 (over 24)	1906 (over 24)	1919	1919
Norway	1907 (over 25)	1907 (over 25)	1919 (over 23)	1919 (over 23)
Denmark		*	1915 (over 25) 1920	1915 (over 25) 1920
Russia		*	1917	1917
UK		1884 (but had to fulfill residential qualification)	1918 (over 30) ‡ 1928 §	1918
Austria		1907	1919	1919
Germany		1871	1919	1919
Czechoslovakia		† (1907)	1919	1919
Netherlands		*	1919	1917
Poland		†	1919	1919
Bulgaria		*	1920	1921
Sweden	1909 (over 24)		1921	1921
Spain		*	1931	
France		1848	1945	
Italy		*	1946	1919
Switzerland		*	1971	
Belgium		*	1948¶	1920

*   limited male franchise based on property.
†   part of one of pre-war empires.
‡   only women aged 30 who were married, householders or university graduates.
§   all women aged 21.
¶   some women obtained the vote in 1920.

From the table you'll see that only in Finland and Norway did *any* European women have the vote in 1914. But these countries were *political* oddities. Norway had only recently gained independence from Sweden, the hegemonic power in Scandinavia. Finland was a duchy within the Russian Empire with a political class which spoke Swedish, not Finnish. The Russian revolution of 1906 swept through the duchy, and on a wave of democratic and nationalist sentiment a unicameral assembly was set up and the vote given to *all* Finns over the age of 24 – the *political* reasoning was that the more voters there were, the stronger the assembly would be against Russian Tsarism. In Norway, one year later, the vote was given to all men and women over 25, who were possessed of a small property qualification (abolished in 1913). The political argument was that women voters would strengthen the nationalist cause against Sweden. As I say in my discussion of this table in Units 7–10:

> One can, I think, make a convincing argument that the *participation* of both the common man and the common woman in the national efforts resulted in women as a sex, and those men previously excluded from the franchise, all getting the vote.
>
> (p.151)

[handwritten margin note: Marwick's claim]

There are certain facts that you must be absolutely sure about: remember that women in both France and Italy did not get the vote at the end of the war. What I suggest is that you now read the extracts I quoted from *Feminism and the Third Republic* by Paul Smith (Units 7–10, pp.154–5).

I shall be discussing high and popular culture, along with film, in a separate section, so I shall move straight to the tenth and last of our areas of possible social change. In 'Institutions and values', I refer back to the exercise chart introduced in Book 1, Unit 4. A chart of this sort is an excellent device for revision. So what I suggest you do now is dig out that chart, and then use it in conjunction with 'Institutions and values', where information is presented in a form that is already highly condensed.

The purpose of this discussion has been to bring to the forefront of your mind the sorts of issues you would need to take up if you were doing an exam question relating to the social consequences of the First World War, or any aspect of them. In dealing, in particular, with social reform, I mentioned the point that sometimes changes seem to be more directly related to the revolutions at the end of the war than to the war itself. Some care is needed in dealing with this. What I recommend is that you clearly single out consequences springing directly from the war experience itself, and distinguish them from consequences resulting from, say, the participation effect, or from the way in which existing institutions and provisions were tested by the war. Then separately (if you agree, that is, that the revolutions themselves were largely products of the war) you can have a list of 'indirect' consequences, consequences of the war which came 'via' the revolutions (new constitutions, new welfare laws, etc.).

3   THE DEBATE OVER THE SOCIAL CONSEQUENCES OF WORLD WAR II

As with the debate over the impact and consequences of World War I, the sorts of questions being asked throughout Book 4, Units 21–25, are:

1   Why did certain developments come about in the way they did and when they did during World War II?

2   What part did the experiences of war play in effecting these changes?

3   What effect did the war have on changes in the post-war period?

4   Did the war speed up, slow down or change the direction of broad movements of socio-economic change?

5   Can we separate out the effects of the war from all the other possible causes of change?

Clearly World War II did not break out in a static world. We need to evaluate the nature and direction of the changes that were taking place in the pre-war years before we can consider changes attributable to the war. You are familiar with Mark Roseman's article (Chapter 14 in the Course Reader), which emphasizes the importance, when evaluating social change in Germany, of taking into account the effects of the six years of Nazi government prior to the war. Nazi policies did much to undermine the class structure of German society and the position of the élite strata. At the same time, the influence of the Soviet Union in East Germany and of the USA in West Germany were obviously crucial in the shaping of post-war German societies. Roseman concludes that, in the German instance, 'total war' is not an independent cause of social change and claims as to its influence need to be seen alongside the influence of the pre-war regime, the specific character of that regime during the war and the nature of regimes which came after the war.

Roseman's article pinpoints two major areas of debate in any discussion concerning World War II. First, by stressing the importance of the Russian and American occupations of Germany, he provides ammunition for those who argue that the major determinant of social change in Europe after 1945 was the division of Europe and the influence of these two major powers. Second, Roseman acknowledges that the experience of Germany was quite different from that of a country such as Britain, where 'the only changes in the political system were those brought about by the needs of war' (Course Reader, p.252).

But what were the effects of the war on Britain? A long-established view is that it radically changed British society and politics. The defeats of 1940 brought down the largely Conservative national government and the formation of Churchill's wartime coalition saw the discrediting not only of the foreign and armaments policies of the pre-war governments but also of their domestic policies. In a sense, the 1930s were discredited and the period became the 'Devil's Decade', a time of wasted opportunities. A new political consensus emerged, one which saw a greater role for the state and central planning, a general acceptance of state-directed social welfare and the view that Keynesian economics could control the economy and limit the oscillations of the free market. The experience of war and the expectations aroused by the Beveridge Report brought about the victory of the Labour Party in the 1945 election and inaugurated six years of radical government, which saw greater state controls, a widened welfare state and the nationalization of basic industries. Even the return of a Conservative government in 1951 and the consequent thirteen years of Conservative rule did not destroy a fundamental consensus for which the term 'Butskellism' was coined (see Paul Addison, *The Road to 1945*, 1975). Revisionist historians have been chipping away at this interpretation, arguing in particular that the extent of political consensus has been much exaggerated (see for instance K. Jefferys, *The Churchill Coalition and Wartime Politics 1940–1945*, 1991), but its influence remains considerable.

To evaluate the long-term influence of the war on Britain, we must, however, have at least some hypothesis as to the direction in which pre-war British society was heading. A re-evaluation of the 1930s has pointed to the rise of a consumer society in which private house building boomed, light industries expanded in the south of England and the sale of electronic goods and motor cars was increasing, while at the same time the heavy industries of the north, Scotland

and Wales declined. It may well be that the most important effect of the war was a temporary reversal of these trends, a revival of heavy industry to cater to the needs of the war economy and a parallel stifling of the emergent economy and society. The post-war Labour government's policies saw this hiatus in the process of development towards a more consumerist, more 'American' society continue into the post-war period, until the developments discernible in the 1930s became once more apparent in the 1950s. This could lead us to conclude that the war's main effect was to retard important socio-economic developments.

What seems undeniable whichever European country we are discussing is that the experience of war had a profound effect. We can argue as to whether it was an independent cause of social change, whether it retarded, speeded up or sidetracked developments and whether its effects were long term or short term, but not that its influence on the lives of whole populations and the direction of economies, both during and after the war, was of no significance.

This leads us to another, if related, area of debate: the effects of mass participation in the war and the need for governments to encourage and direct that participation. The eminent military historian Michael Howard has argued that:

> The Second World War awoke a new interest in the relationship between war and social change. Not only did it accelerate within all the societies involved, the processes of change catalysed by the Great War, but it brought social involvement in belligerent activity to a new level of intensity by eliminating the distinction between 'front line' and 'base'. This distinction had characterised not only the 1914–18 war but the great majority of wars in Europe since the seventeenth century.
>
> (Michael Howard, 'Total war in the twentieth century: participation and consensus in the Second World War', 1976, pp.216–17)

It is important to bear in mind these two areas of debate while examining the particular areas of change discussed in Units 21–25.

Social geography

In the medium term the war had an enormous impact on the social geography of Europe. There was a greater loss of life than in World War I, with countries in eastern, central and southern Europe suffering most severely. In addition, there were vast movements of population within Europe, starting with the 'New Order' aims of Germany and the resettlement plans of the Soviet Union in the early years of the war, and culminating in the transfer of some 6 million Germans back to Germany in the aftermath of 1945. In all, movements of population for ideological reasons and because of frontier changes involved some 25 million people during and immediately after the war.

Although there were higher marriage and fertility rates in western Europe in the post-war period compared with the interwar years, immigration (especially immigration into West Germany) was the major reason for the increase in the population of western Europe.

Economic performance and theory

Again as in World War I, the economies of the European powers were diverted from traditional areas of production towards wartime economies. In this respect Britain and Russia, in Roberts's words, 'achieved the greatest subordination of economy and society to the war effort' (p.445). The Soviet Union had, so I have argued, a virtual war economy before 1939. State resources were already focused on heavy industrial production and armaments, so that by 1940 the state budget directed to armaments alone was 32.6 per cent. In Britain the politicians drew upon the experiences of central planning learned in World War I. Coal mines, shipping and railways were put under state control, and 'The government moved in a corporatist direction as Bevin attempted to enlist the support of trade union leaders for the direction and allocation of labour' (Book 4, Units 21–25, p.82).

Compared with Britain the 'totalitarian' state of Germany did not achieve anything like this degree of economic mobilization until well towards the end of the war. The reasons why Germany did not undergo central planning to the extent of that experienced in Britain is well explained in Roberts, page 446, and the Roseman article already mentioned above. (Note, however, that the article by Richard Overy in the Course Reader challenges some of these assumptions.)

In World War I, France, Belgium and Serbia in particular suffered devastation and a vast destruction of property. Between 1939 and 1945 the arena of war ranged far more widely and, consequently, devastation was more general. By the end of the war all the European countries faced, in varying degrees, formidable economic problems: food shortages, dislocation of industrial production, lost export markets, the liquidation of overseas investments and inflation.

Nevertheless, as I've suggested, 'The infrastructure of the European economy had been damaged but not destroyed by the war' (Units 21–25, p.90), and the preconditions for industrial recovery in Europe were present. With financial assistance coming from the United States, within five years of the ending of the war, 'European output of almost everything was to be substantially above pre-war levels'. Although, partly as a result of the war, Europe's trading and financial position declined in importance relative to the world economy, 'in absolute terms it not only remained dynamic and sophisticated but had considerable potential for expansion' (Units 21–25, p.78).

National cohesion

Clearly nationality and race were prominent issues in World War II. Nazi notions of racial purity, *Herrenvolk, Untermenschen* and anti-Semitism, together with the aim to unite all Germans under one great empire, eventually involved not only a holocaust but vast movements of people throughout central and eastern Europe. This, together with Russia's territorial ambitions and other national rivalries within Czechoslovakia, Hungary and Yugoslavia in particular, meant that nationality was a significant issue before, during and after the war.

Arthur Marwick concludes that 'On the whole it could be said that the general movement which had accelerated earlier in the century towards each nationality having its own nation-state was consolidated in the aftermath of World War II' (Units 21–25, p.114). But as he states, this consolidation was achieved at a brutal human cost. The end of the Second World War saw a ruthless compression of peoples into new frontiers, which were more firmly aligned with ethnic divisions. As I described this in Book 4:

> Germans were pushed westwards and their place was taken by Poles and Czechs; Poles and Czechs were in their turn pushed westwards and their place was taken by Russians. There were exchanges of population between Czechoslovakia and Hungary and between Hungary and Yugoslavia. Well over 200,000 Italians left territory gained by Yugoslavia, while 103,000 Hungarians were repatriated from Romania.
>
> (Units 21–25, p.75)

Class

In section 2 of Units 21–25 (in the sub-section 'Social structure'), Arthur Marwick considers, in considerable detail, whether the experiences of the war did or did not result in changes in social structures and the relationships between the attitudes towards classes. In the case of Britain, he examines critically an important article, 'The "levelling of class"', by Penny Summerfield. In this article Summerfield argues that in Britain there was very little sign, if any, of social levelling during the period 1939–45. If you wish to refresh your memory, read the last four paragraphs of her article (on pages 216–17 of the Course Reader), where she sets out her main conclusions. Arthur Marwick contests these conclusions and, although he argues that the phrases 'levelling' and 'social mixing' are unsatisfactory, he contends that they refer to something that did occur to some extent. 'The working class in general gained in living conditions and in self-confidence; it was treated less contemptuously by members of other social classes' (Units 21–25, p.102). Tony Aldgate, in his study of British cinema during the war years, supports this view. He points out that there was a new emphasis on the part played by working men and women within society. 'Working-class figures were given a fuller and more rounded characterization' and, in addition, 'subjects were broached in the cinema, as on radio, that had been barely touched upon before' (Units 21–25, p.183).

Turning to France, Arthur Marwick explores the notion of whether 'participation' resulted in social gains and he relates this especially to those who participated in the Resistance. He concludes that the experiences of the Resistance did result in social mixing, although he admits that until the last year of the war, the Resistance involved only about 4 per cent of the population. Overall, he concludes that in the longer term the effects of World War II on the working class in France were similar to those in Britain. 'The working class did not change its position in the hierarchy, but it benefited from the social legislation introduced after the war' (Units 21–25, p.105). Also there were 'changes *within* the upper class, much greater recruitment from below, and perhaps quite far below compared with Britain, taking into consideration the strongly working-class composition of the Resistance' (Units 21–25, p.106).

In the section on France, Arthur Marwick draws upon Stanley Hoffman's article 'The effects of World War II on French society and politics' in the Course Reader. He refers to Hoffman's contention that the French social system begins to change around 1934 (echoes of the Roseman article), but that the old system only disappears with the war itself. Again, it is worth referring back to the final pages of the article (Course Reader, pp.193–5), where Hoffman summarizes his arguments, one of which is that 'the two groups which gained most from the war years were business and the Catholic Church'.

With Italy, as with France, Arthur Marwick explores working-class participation. 'It is a moot point whether (mainly non-violent) resistance to Mussolini, or the military resistance to the German occupation which took over in the north of Italy in September 1943 ... were more important in stimulating social change at the end of the war'. Overall he concludes that 'As elsewhere, then, the story is of general working-class gains (though intense privation after 1943) within a basically unaltered class structure. Wartime conditions were again favourable for the peasants who, as in France, could keep their food to themselves or put it on the black market' (Units 21–25, p.107).

Mark Roseman's thesis outlined in his article 'World War II and social change in Germany' has already been touched on. He argues that social changes and changes in class relationships were already taking place before the war in Nazi Germany. The war continued this social mobility, and after the war the Allies played a significant role in ensuring industrial harmony. While Arthur Marwick questions the extent of the influence of the Allies in this respect, he does agree with Roseman that what emerged 'was a hard-working, consumer-oriented, sceptical and unpolitical working class. A strong suspicion of the bosses coexisted with the feeling that labour's status had collectively improved' (Course Reader, p.251).

Less change took place in the social structure of Russia than in any of the other major powers, and Paul Dukes, cited by Arthur Marwick, has argued that any chances of change within Russian society were ended by the Cold War. (Dukes's article is in *Total War and Social Change*, edited by Arthur Marwick, 1988.)

Social policy and social welfare

In his discussion of the impact of World War I on social change, Arthur Marwick drew up a league table of countries in which there was the most social legislation during and after the war. If he had done the same for the period of World War II, Britain again would have headed the list. A spate of social legislation towards the end of the war and during the period of the post-war Labour government affected all sections of British society. The 1944 Education Act, the 1945 Family Allowance Act, the 1946 Acts involving National Insurance, Industrial Injuries and the National Health Service, and the National Assistance Act of 1948, all played their part in establishing what came to be known as the British welfare state. Some of this legislation was based on and influenced by the Beveridge Report, which was first published in December 1942. Arthur Marwick concentrates much of his discussion on this Report with its 'comprehensive policy of social progress' in order to argue that a document produced during the early years of the war must form 'a vital link in any chain joining the war experience to the enactment of social legislation. It also had symbolic significance when resistance fighters and progressive elements in other countries discussed the kind of society there should be after the war' (Units 21–25, p.120).

After Britain, it was France, ahead of Germany and Russia among the leading powers, which was most affected by the new welfare legislation. A number of important ordinances relating to social security were established in 1944 and 1945, some of which were based on the proposals expounded in the Programme of the National Council of Resistance and first published in 1944. If you turn back to Book 1, Unit 1, you will see it argued that the significance of this programme, drawn up by a body consisting of resistance groups of various political viewpoints, 'is that it shows the experience of war (specifically of Resistance) engendering ideas of consensus on behalf of progressive economic and social planning. Because of the prestige of the Resistance, and because of the feeling that defeated France had been a flop, many of these proposals were put into practice after the Liberation' (p.22).

Material conditions

In considering material conditions, it is important to differentiate between the immediate and the long-term effects of the war. As Arthur Marwick and I both point out, recovery from the war came relatively quickly. However, as Arthur Marwick shows, in Poland, where 18 per cent of the population was killed, and Russia and Yugoslavia, where over 11 per cent of the population died in each country, material conditions during the war were dire in the extreme. In Germany and Italy conditions deteriorated rapidly from 1943 onwards. While the black market flourished in Italy, the amount of food available for most Italians was significantly reduced. Prices in 1945 were twenty-four times above those existing in 1938, and income per head of the population was lower than it had been in 1861.

Both Britain and France suffered fewer casualties in World War II than in World War I. Only 0.9 per cent of Britain's population was killed compared with 7.4 for that of Germany. Although food was comparatively scarce, the rationing system in Britain ensured a fairer distribution of food and 'for many families, higher nutrition standards than had obtained before the war' (Units 21–25, p.127).

Customs and behaviour

Customs and behaviour might well have been influenced during the course of the war, so Arthur Marwick argues, in two major ways. Firstly as a result of the vast shifts of population and the changes in class relations. Secondly through the violence and disruption which accompanies wars and which affects civic morality. He notes, in relation to the first point, that there was 'less formality, less sense of hierarchy in most countries', but with regard to the second, 'civic norms were in fact established remarkably quickly' (Units 21–25, p.133).

As to whether American involvement in Europe during and immediately following the war led to a marked acceptance of American customs and patterns of behaviour, he argues that some commentators have over-emphasized American influence. In making your own judgement on this matter it is worth referring again to the discussion of Document II.32 in *Primary Sources 2: Interwar and World War II*, 'An average French town in 1950' (in Units 21–25, pp.162–4).

The changes in customs and behaviour that occurred during World War II which Arthur Marwick regards as significant are:

1   developments in religion, especially the political role of Christian Democracy in West Germany and Italy, and the essentially Christian Democrat MRP (Popular Republican Movement) in France; in Russia, the Russian Orthodox Church, by supporting the government during the war, was granted in return 'the right to exist as an institution in Soviet society' (Units 21–25, p.134);

2   the popularizing of radio as a means of communication in conveying both news and entertainment.

Women and the family

Arthur Marwick argues that in Britain the war brought new employment opportunities for married women in particular, and it helped to break down the prejudices against married women taking jobs.

> The conclusion is inescapable that the Second World War offered women opportunities normally unavailable in peace time to improve their economic and social status, and to develop their own confidence and self-consciousness. In many cases these opportunities were firmly grasped; whether they would be extended depended very much on women themselves, for, without doubt, old attitudes, overpoweringly strong in 1941 [or 1939], were still influential in 1946.
>
> (Arthur Marwick, *War and Social Change in the Twentieth Century*, 1974, p.175; quoted in Units 21–25, pp.135–6)

British films, such as *The Gentle Sex* and *Millions Like Us*, emphasized the important wartime roles that women were playing, and many other wartime sources suggest a consciousness that there was a change in the status of women. We must remember, however, that such films were concerned to suggest, in the interests of morale and the war effort, that such changes were welcomed. We must not assume that all unmarried women welcomed the limitations on their freedom that came with conscription for the war effort or the new roles they were called upon to perform. The Ministry of Information and the film-makers it commissioned had a propaganda message to put over: the country needed women to perform non-traditional roles and the women, supposedly, relished their new roles. Some, undoubtedly, did.

Contrast this attitude with that of German film-makers who, so the leading authority, David Welch, contends in *Propaganda and the German Cinema 1933–1945* (1983), represented women only in the roles of wives and mothers. This fits in with Roseman's point that many Nazi leaders were reluctant to involve women in the wartime economy: 'the number of German women in the economy actually fell between 1939 and 1941 and in 1942 was still lower than in the pre-war period. Whereas in 1943 almost two-thirds of British women were in employment, the equivalent figure for Germany was only 46 per cent' (Course Reader, p.242). (Richard Overy has challenged some of these views – see Arthur Marwick's discussion in the Introduction to Units 21–25.)

Whether women's work in the resistance movements led to social promotion is a moot point. François Bédarida, although pointing out that French women finally were enfranchised in 1944, is doubtful whether they made any other gains. However, Arthur Marwick quotes Tannenbaum, who argues that in Italy 'the active role played by women in the Resistance helped to change the status of women as a whole in the post-war period' (*The Fascist Experience*, 1972, p.323; quoted in Units 21–25, p.138).

In Russia where, as Arthur Marwick points out, one would expect equal rights for women, the chances of reaching the upper echelons of political power were small indeed. In 1942, there were only two women representatives among the 125 full members of the Central Committee. But, quoting Dukes, he indicates an improvement over the war period.

High culture and popular culture

In section 3 of Units 21–25, Tony Aldgate and James Chapman stress the importance of film and radio both as instruments of propaganda and as entertainment. After the war in France, as Document II.32 in *Primary Sources 2: Interwar and World War II*, points out, cinema-going was the favourite leisure activity and the public preferred French to American films. Arthur Marwick also argues that in France, Italy and Britain, film-makers developed their own traditions and that Americanization was not as powerful an influence as has often been suggested. With regard to high culture, the

> catastrophe of the First World War did have profound effects on the subject matter, beliefs and modes of expression of artists and thinkers. The Second World War came to a much less naïve world, and therefore did not have the same effect in transforming modes of thought and expression. It was, nonetheless, an experience of enormous intensity, and resulted in the production of a considerable body of work related directly to that experience. It can indeed be argued that while the trauma of World War I turned intellectuals in on themselves and towards the esoteric modes of modernism, World War II, as a war of peoples and partisans, induced a turning back towards realism.
>
> (Units 21–25, p.147)

Political institutions and values

In Units 21–25, section 2 (in the sub-section 'Political institutions and values'), Arthur Marwick surveys each of the major powers in turn. He argues that in Britain during the war there was a growing desire for social change. In section 3 Tony Aldgate and James Chapman add to this view by stressing that this 'popular feeling' was one of resentment against vested interests and privileges and a wish for general improvements after the war, rather than a strong political expression. However, they do agree with Arthur Marwick that the return of a Labour government was directly connected with the war experience and the desire for social change. As mentioned earlier in this unit and as I suggest in section 2 of Units 21–25 (in the sub-section 'Social geography'), I would largely concur that these were indeed the immediate effects of the war. I would, however, argue that there was much less of a consensus than has been suggested, that the desire for social benefits was based on an illusory view of Britain's economic position, and that the direction of post-war policies was an interruption to the long-term developments in the British economy and British society.

In France, despite arguments that the spirit of change engendered by the Resistance soon disappeared, Arthur Marwick maintains that the reconstruction of the French civil service enabled the development of vigorous planning and economic initiatives in the post-war years. We should not, however, forget Hoffman's view (in the article reproduced in the Course Reader) that there was considerable continuity between pre-war, Vichy and post-war developments, a continuity extending to the very personnel who made up the politicians and technocrats of these regimes.

Italy, so Arthur Marwick argues, underwent the most marked political changes of all the western powers. The democratic system of government was vastly different in the post-war years from the Italy of pre-1914 or the years of Mussolini's rule. The Christian Democrats dominated the political scene, but the Italian Communist Party was influential in many parts of Italy. The pattern of a dominant Christian Democracy facing a challenge from communism, with a number of socialist, radical and *right-of-centre* parties often holding the balance, was to be a constant of Italian politics for decades.

In divided Germany, both the western powers and the Soviet Union were determined that there be a clear break with the Nazi past, but the policies adopted in the zones occupied by the western Allies were very different to those implemented in the Soviet zone. The Soviet authorities sought to change the whole structure of society as well as its economic base. There was an administrative purge, which targeted not only Nazis but also those who could be deemed potential enemies of socialism, while new personnel were trained. Perhaps more important was economic revolution involving the expropriation of landed estates, banks and heavy industry. By the end of 1946, the eastern zone was virtually a one-party socialist state. In the western zones there were judicial investigations of those with Nazi pasts on a case-by-case basis, a process which soon broke down in the light of the millions of cases to be investigated. Not being committed to a total reordering of the economy and society, the western Allies sought rather to encourage democratic forces and by a process of education denazify the population. The western Allies played an important role in ensuring the eventual emergence of a German democratic system dominated by the Christian Democratic Party. Their other goals were economic recovery and social stability – to have dismissed every schoolteacher, professor or judge with a Nazi past or confiscated the businesses of every industrialist who had co-operated with the Nazi regime would have impeded both aims. In terms of the fabric of social and economic life, as opposed to political life, there was, therefore, considerable continuity.

Conclusion

In section 3 of Units 21–25, Tony Aldgate and James Chapman analysed the problems facing the European powers in a war which had no 'front line' or 'base'. How in the face of bombing, evacuation and hardship was the consensus for waging the war to be maintained? Did this mean, as Arthur Marwick has maintained, that societies were 'tested' and that the relationships between leaders and led had to be reformulated?

After reading Units 21–25 it is up to you to decide whether there were signs of change in the relations between the leaders and the led as a result of the war experience. The units have explored ten vital areas in which social change may or may not have occurred, and you must assess the often conflicting arguments of historians like Arthur Marwick, who contends that, in a variety of ways, World War II did bring social changes, and those like Angus Calder, whom Tony Aldgate and James Chapman quote, who argues that in Britain at least, 'The effect of the war was not to sweep society on to a new course, but to hasten its progress along the old grooves' (Calder, *The People's War*, 1969, p.20; quoted in Units 21–25, p.182). As I've previously said, my own opinion is that the war's effect on Britain was to temporarily divert it from the direction in which it was moving in the 1930s. Any generalization about its effects upon European society (east and west) is bold.

Whatever your conclusions, Europe in 1945 was a vastly different place from the Europe we examined at the start of the course. As Roberts points out:

> Europe's self-inflicted wounds had all but destroyed her ... At the moment, it was hard even to detect a glow in the ashes; the economic resurgence of the next quarter-century could no more be anticipated than the shape of new political structures which was to accompany it. All that was certain was that a dream which had haunted the interwar years had been blown to the winds; there could be no return to 1914. It was at last clearly impossible.
>
> (Roberts, p.463)

4   WOMEN, MEN, GENDER AND WAR

One of the main themes of this course has been to explore the impact of the total wars of the twentieth century on the role and status of women. While the extent to which economic, political and social equality has been achieved between the sexes remains contested, few could seriously doubt that there has been significant change in the role and status of women in Europe during the twentieth century. The question posed in this course is, how much of this change has been generated by war? My intention here is twofold: I want to assist your revision first, by rehearsing some of the evidence already discussed in the course, and second, by encouraging you to think about that evidence again, critically and comparatively.

Much of the recent research into the working-class family at the close of the nineteenth and beginning of the twentieth centuries has stressed the developing notions of respectability, which included the male breadwinner's ability to keep his family on his own, single wage while his wife kept the home and looked after the children. The harsh realities of life may not have allowed the achievement of this aspiration, but how far war undermined it between 1914 and 1918 and again between 1939 and 1945 remains an open question. Few of the men who went to war in 1914 or 1939 saw themselves serving as soldiers, sailors or airmen after the war; by the same token, why should the women who replaced them in the economy or who took new jobs in war industries such as munitions production have considered themselves as earning a living in this way after the war? Of course, horizons may have been broadened, aspirations may have been enhanced or enlarged, but proving such broadening, enhancement or enlargement within social groups, and then determining the cause, is never a particularly easy task for the historian.

Arthur Marwick and others have argued that women's participation in the war efforts in Britain contributed to their political enfranchisement after World War I and to their increasing economic independence. But the impact of war was not the same across all social groups and all kinds of trade and profession. The long-term trend in women's employment in the first half of the twentieth century, namely a growth in the 'white-blouse' labour force and a decline in female factory labour, was becoming apparent before 1914. Some women did acquire new labour skills and follow new forms of employment during both world wars, and some were reluctant to surrender these with the return of peace. Finding young women prepared to act as live-in domestic servants in the aftermath of World War I might be taken as an indicator of new horizons for young women. Yet there were plenty of domestic servants to be found during the 1920s and 1930s, indeed the numbers increased from 1.072 million in 1921 to 1.262 million ten years later. Increasingly, however, they chose not to live in the house of their employer.

There are also questions to be posed about any notion of a simple equation suggesting that women's participation in war led to female political enfranchisement. The election of December 1910 had produced a House of Commons in favour of extending the vote to women. In July 1911 the Parliamentary Franchise (Women) Bill passed its second reading by 299 votes to 189, but got no further since Asquith's government would not find the necessary parliamentary time. Moreover, young unmarried women, temporarily drawn into engineering and munitions during the war, were not among the women enfranchised in 1918.

Martin Pugh has suggested that the suffragettes' commitment to the war effort may, in fact, have set back the moment when the vote was achieved (*Women and the Women's Movement in Britain, 1914–1959*, 1992). Susan Kingsley Kent has taken a rather different, but similarly revisionist, perspective, suggesting that the war fostered a new kind of feminism which insisted that conflict, violence and war might best be avoided in future by reasserting the 'gendered spheres of public and private' (Kent, 'The politics of sexual difference: World War One and the demise of British feminism', 1988, p.253). For Kent, World War I proved to be something of a check to women's progress and feminist ideas in Britain, and it took a second war to restore the situation and pave the way for significant advances, which only really came in the 1960s (Kent, *Making Peace: The Reconstruction of Gender in Interwar Britain*, 1993).

The French evidence shows women participating in the national effort of 1914–18 in ways similar to women in Britain. But, again, long-term trends complicate any simple conclusion about the impact of war on women's labour. The ratio of working women to working men declined between 1906 and 1926, which is not the situation that would automatically be expected given the numbers of men killed during the war. The reason for this appears to be the huge increase in marriages after 1919. Much of this was because marriages were delayed during the war, but the marriage rate during the 1920s remained higher than it had been before the war, and married women went out to work less frequently than spinsters (the same was true in Britain).

The question of votes for women in France is equally complex. Though not without opposition, women seemed to have been making significant strides towards enfranchisement before the war; they had, for example, acquired some voting rights for the *Conseils des Prud'hommes* and were moving into some professions (Book 1, Unit 2, p.55). Steven C. Hause has argued that French feminists were so sure of getting the vote at the end of the war that they did not bother campaigning for it in 1919, preferring to concentrate on explaining the political process to women (Hause, 'More Minerva than Mars: the French Women's Rights Campaign and the First World War', 1987). But there was no political enfranchisement when peace came. Following the logic of the British experience this seems odd; but the logic of one country's experience does not automatically hold good for another. While historians have described World War I as a stimulus to enfranchisement and increasing economic independence in Britain, others have described it as having precisely the opposite effect in France. Michelle Perrot, for example, has pointed to powerful attacks on feminism during the war. The old gender roles were given a new emphasis, with men required to fulfil the public duty of fighting for the motherland, while women's duty was domestic, protecting the home and nurturing children (Perrot, 'The New Eve and the Old Adam: changes in French women's condition at the turn of the century', 1987). Such ideas can be seen reflected strongly in wartime popular literature. In ... *puis il mourut* (1916), for example, the novelist Jeanne Landre has the hero writing from the trenches to his love: 'during this time make yourself beautiful and desirable for the return of the victor'; after the battle she would be his '*superbe compensation*' (quoted in C. O'Brien, 'Beyond the can[n]on: French women's responses to the First World War', 1996, p.205).

Arthur Marwick has never proposed the simple equation: women's participation in war led to political enfranchisement in Britain. Similarly Michelle Perrot has never proposed the simple equation: war led to a revival and strengthening of old-style paternalism in France and therefore women's suffrage was checked. However, both have described the war as influential in the subsequent, contrasting development of women's suffrage in the two countries. In section 2 of this unit you will find a table listing the dates of the first legislation conceding men's and women's franchise in national (as opposed to municipal) elections in selected European countries. It should at least make you ponder the role of war in influencing events in Britain, especially when you consider that two White Dominions of the British Empire, New Zealand and Australia, enfranchised women respectively in 1893 and 1901. Might this not suggest a trend in the Empire? And if there were a series of countries introducing women's suffrage in the aftermath of both world wars, might this be as much a determination to break with the past regime and an expression of faith in the future with a system which, in the aftermath of war and, in many instances revolution or national independence, was considered to be new, reformed and modernized? The clearest example of this is revolutionary Russia where women were rapidly emancipated to an unprecedented extent. Yet in the early years of the Soviet Union much of the emancipation was regarded with considerable suspicion by working-class and peasant women, who saw liberal divorce laws as a way for men to escape their responsibilities towards wives and children, feared that the ideas of free love and of free unions between men and women would essentially be of benefit only to men, and who continued to favour traditional ideas of marriage and the gendered divisions of labour and household management. By the mid-1930s Stalin was also concerned about the effects of the libertarian ideas in encouraging divorce and abortion; as a result, a new policy of commitment to the traditional family was proclaimed, replacing the liberal Bolshevik laws.

Women were called upon to work in factories and transport systems, replacing men serving at the front, in most of the major combatant countries during World War I. Holger Herwig paints a grim picture of those employed in factories in Germany:

> While women's average daily earnings rose by 138 per cent – compared with 112 for men – during the war, they were paid 63 to 71 per cent less than males in electrical, chemical and machine industries. Daily wages of between 1.45 and 2.40 Marks barely covered food costs of roughly 2 Marks. Seventy per cent of female factory workers put in between 51 and 60 hours per week and almost 30 per cent between 66 and 75. Night work doubled during the war ... Poisons used in the manufacture of shells and canisters reduced the birthrate among women in armaments plants by half. No statistics seem to have been kept on birth defects as a result of these toxins in the workplace.
>
> (Herwig, *The First World War*, 1997, p.295)

As well as factory work the war also brought a big growth in traditional out-work in Germany, that is work done by women in their homes – the place where, as a good wife and mother, traditionally they were expected to be, and where, quite probably as a wife and mother, they wanted to be. Membership of the Women Homeworkers' Union increased from 8,385 in 1913 to 19,644 in January 1919; and while work was done at home, much of it was specifically war work, making covers for gun parts, baskets to pass ammunition, uniforms, belts, gasmasks, sandbags (Daniel, 'Women's work in industry and family: Germany 1914–1918', 1988, p.277).

In 'Italian peasant women and the First World War' (Chapter 5 in the Course Reader), Anna Bravo has described women peasants in Italy finding themselves forced to negotiate with representatives of the state in the absence of their menfolk at the front. While, with peace, things largely returned to the way they had been, nevertheless, she suggests, a 'venthole had been opened, which could not be wholly closed' (Course Reader, p.96). The same might be said for the experience of women elsewhere. If nothing else, they often had to secure for themselves such allowances as they were permitted as wives or mothers of serving soldiers. They also had to plan the family budget; this was not necessarily a new thing, but wartime inflation and food shortages brought considerable complications and, for women in towns, could necessitate hours of queuing, trips to the country to secure produce, or finding black-market outlets. Such tasks could increase self-confidence and self-awareness; the question is to assess how this may have influenced women, particularly working-class women, as a social group. Did their daughters not have to go through a similar experience twenty years later, facing essentially the same prejudices in the workplace and from officialdom?

The problems of inflation, low pay and shortages may have encouraged some women into prostitution. Large numbers of young men cooped up in barracks and preparing for the slaughterhouse of the front provided a ready market. It has been estimated that 35,000 women worked as prostitutes in Vienna alone during World War I, charging each client between 20 and 40 Kronen; the food and cost-of-living supplement for the female head of a household in Innsbruck in February 1915 was 1.5 Kronen (Herwig, *The First World War*, 1997, p.282). In December 1918 the Reich Office for Economic Demobilization in Germany was concerned that women who had been engaged in war work would now slip into prostitution, thus heightening 'the danger of infection and of moral decay' especially around transit camps for the returning troops (Bessel, *Germany after the First World War*, 1993, p.235). Perhaps it hardly needs noting that in the perception of the (male) bureaucrats in this office it was the prostitutes (women) who would be spreading 'infection' and 'moral decay' rather than the returning soldiers. European feminists had long protested about legal systems in which the prostitute was subject to inspection and in which soliciting was a criminal offence, but there were no sanctions against the male client. The war had not changed matters. Moreover, while the war may well have encouraged a greater degree of sexual freedom among courting couples fearing that a soldier might never return, how far might the awareness and criticism of changing sexual mores have been moulded rather more by concerns about a visible growth in prostitution around military camps, and greatly expanded garrisons and naval dockyards? In Britain, for example, it was the 'loose' or 'giddy' young woman who was commonly described as a threat to the soldiery, rather than vice versa; wartime legislation seeking to prevent the spread of venereal disease among the armed forces singled out the infected woman, who was to be named and shamed, while male accusers maintained their anonymity (P. Levine, 'Rough usage: prostitution, law and the social historian', 1993).

During World War I it was urged in many combatant countries that pregnancy was the woman's active service, and, partly as a consequence of the losses sustained in the war, such notions continued across Europe throughout the interwar period. At the same time they also harkened back to the concerns about 'the race' which were to be found in several of the great powers before 1914 (Book 1, Unit 2, pp.70–1); 'tell the women I need births, many births' Mussolini instructed the heads of Fascist women's organizations (quoted in V. de Grazia, *How Fascism Ruled Women: Italy, 1922–1945*, 1992, p.25). This sort of thinking was not confined to the revolutionary right of the interwar and Second World War periods, but it did find its most powerful articulation among the Fascist and Nazi ideologues. These ideologues had, however, failed to understand the experience of World War I and to think through the logic of their policies. If a woman's place was in the home, breeding and nurturing little warriors, who was going to fill in for the big warriors when war took them away from the fields, the factories, the transport systems and the administration of their modern societies? In June 1940 Mussolini's regime reversed its pre-war policy of seeking to exclude women from the labour market and directed that they be allowed to replace men in public administration now called up for war service. At the same time women began replacing men similarly called up from the large industrial enterprises of Milan and Turin. Hitler was less easy to move in these respects. Slave labour and prisoners of war could be used before German women; and Hitler even suggested to his subordinates that they import as workers Ukrainian women or 'dumpy, primitive and healthy Russian women' before calling upon slender Aryan German women (quoted in J. Noakes, 'Germany', 1992, p.44). However, from 1943 in particular, Nazi Germany began to reverse its pre-war policy of discriminating against women in the workplace. This was most notable in the case of women in professional careers. In authorizing the acceptance of more women students to train for such careers, the regime saw itself as preparing for the future; these women would be needed until a new post-war generation of male students could be trained. In Vichy France women and the family were idealized in propaganda, and women in the Resistance used this to their own advantage, travelling 'confidently through the public spaces and across huge distances':

> Shopping baskets and bags, children's necessities and equipment of all kinds, and the proprieties of imminent or recent motherhood, provided a cover for transportation and movement sanctified by the familial and natalist priorities of the regime
>
> (H. R. Kedward, *In Search of the Maquis: Rural Resistance in Southern France 1942–1944*, 1993, p.90)

But whether women's participation in the war efforts of Fascist Italy and Nazi Germany and in the French, and other, Resistance movements had any positive outcome in changing the role and status of women over time is difficult to estimate. Kedward doubts that the degree of egalitarianism found within the French Resistance 'brought substantial changes in the sexual politics within French society' (p.94). As for change in post-war Germany and Italy, any that can be identified might be put down to a desire to break with the previous regime. Moreover, passing a law to establish economic, political or social equality does not guarantee that such a law will be enforced in the spirit apparently intended. Nor should it be inferred that the end of an oppressive regime means an end to all of its legislation, even that which, in retrospect, we might consider repressive. The Nazi prohibition of the sale of contraceptives was not removed in West Germany until 1961; it was another ten years before similar Fascist legislation was removed in Italy; and France removed similar prohibitions only in 1967.

Two other important points need to be made with reference to women on continental Europe during World War II, and these take us far from the comfortable notions of war as contributing to progressive economic, political or social change. First, the heroic image of Resistance had obscured the scale of collaboration in Nazi-occupied Europe. The number of women in France who had their heads shaved, or worse, during the Liberation, accused of *collaboration horizontale*, has never been computed. Probably at least as many actively collaborated – and not just sexually – as resisted. Vast numbers of women in the occupied regions of the USSR participated in sexual relationships with Germans – often, it seems, simply to get food. When partisans or Red Army troops reoccupied the territory such women were commonly shot. Second, defeat and occupation for women in East Prussia, Pomerania and Silesia in 1945 commonly meant mass rape by Red Army soldiers. The number of women victims of these rapes ran, at least, into hundreds of thousands.

As for British society, the kinds of debates which have emerged around the impact of World War II on the position of women are much the same as those which emerged around the impact of World War I. There is what we might call the optimistic view, which sees war as contributing to greater independence for women. Yet Harold Smith has concluded that 'the war's most important legacy was a strengthening of traditional sex roles rather than the emergence of new roles' (Smith, 'The effect of war on the status of women', 1986, p.225); and, in her highly regarded study of women workers during the war, Penny Summerfield considered that 'in spite of the challenge and expectation of change during the war, continuity with pre-war attitudes and practices towards women was considerable in areas of both domestic and paid employment' (Summerfield, *Women Workers in the Second World War*, 1989, p.1). Summerfield begins a later book by recounting how, towards the end of the 1970s, she had talked about her research to a Workers' Educational Association meeting, arguing that the war had done little to alter the sexual division of labour and stressing that women had not shown much identification with war work; these conclusions had drawn heavily on a Mass-Observation report, *War Factory*, published in 1943. She goes on to explain how two women in the audience, who had done war work, strongly criticized her in the light of their personal experiences, and this criticism led to a subsequent study based on oral interviews. Here Summerfield seeks to draw distinctions between the differing perceptions of different women who lived through World War II, and she presents the reader with a variety of individual perspectives which make perfect sense to the individuals concerned, but which, at times, can seem contradictory as a whole (Summerfield, *Reconstructing Women's Wartime Lives*, 1998). But that, of course, is the nature of history.

5   WAR, THE ARTS AND FILM (WITH SOME COMMENTS ON RADIO)

In the long TMA which you prepare at Residential School, we give you the chance to specialize either in film or in the arts. In the exam there might be a question linking the two, or there might be two separate questions. If you are one of the many students a little afraid of the arts, remember that no special 'theory' is required: you are being invited to apply historical methods to a particularly interesting range of materials. To provide for effective revision in short space, I am going to work through a list of the sorts of issues that come up when we think, either singly or together, about war and the arts and war and film. I shall try to keep making comparative points throughout, though these are intended only to stimulate your own thinking – they are not meant to be 'correct' answers ready for transcription into your exam paper.

Usefulness as sources for the study of total war and social change

Probably the reaction of most people would be: 'Of course, film is much more useful than the arts.' But this is where the special 'intermediate' position of literature comes in: war novels, such as *All Quiet on the Western Front*, surely form as direct a source as any film? So, right away, as in any other exam question, be poised to break the question down into its component parts.

Separate out (depending on the wording of the question, naturally) literature from music and art, and then separate these two from each other. Perhaps separate literature into popular literature and élite literature, or perhaps into novels and poetry. Perhaps have separate headings for 'popular art' (you have the posters, and some illustrations in the units) and 'élite art' (discussed on the audio), and between 'popular music' and 'élite music'. (For popular music you have some extracts from Vera Lynn at the end of Audio 4, and you may well know popular songs from both wars. What we have taught you in this course is a methodology which *you* can apply to materials brought in from outside the course: but don't just throw in names – of songs, etc. – without making relevant comments on them.) With film, it is very important to make distinctions between feature films, documentaries and newsreels.

With regard to this last point, probably the obvious reaction would be that newsreel certainly, and documentaries probably, would contain more hard information for historians. But then would we really go to newsreels and documentaries for hard information? An important consideration always to keep in mind when dealing with questions in this general area is that historians should always go to the *best* source for whatever particular type of information it is that they are after. For hard information – number of aeroplanes built, number of calories consumed, complete texts of speeches – it will almost always be better to go to written sources, statistical tables, etc. What films are principally valuable for are attitudes and values, assumptions and aspirations. Thus there may not, after all, be *such* a difference in what historians glean from 'factual' (!) and feature films. In Book 2, Units 7–10, section 3, James Chapman raises the very pertinent question of how film can be used as a primary source. *La Grande Illusion*, taken within the context of how it was received by audiences at the time (one can never fully make use of a primary source without taking it within its context), is an excellent source for 'attitudes' (broadly against war and for peace) in the 1930s. And it is an excellent primary source for 'perceptions of the First World War' as seen from the 1930s. The film also suggests many things about the effects of the First World War on class structure and class relationships. What Jean Renoir (the film's director) suggests is very shrewd, but here the film does not have the status of a primary source. What *is* a primary source in this respect is the novel *Under Fire*, published in 1916, which gives us, filtered through the intellect and literary style of Henri Barbusse, of course, an expression of the sentiments of ordinary soldiers. Being published in 1915 the novel can only hint at changes perhaps beginning to take place: it is not a source for what actually did happen – for that we would need primary sources from the interwar years.

The first examples of film you looked at were extracts from newsreels of 1914 showing troops leaving Britain, France and Turkey for the front. Remind yourself of the very cautious assessment made of them by James Chapman (Units 7–10, pp.183–4). Staying with the question of the unwitting testimony that can come through in film material, I am going to quote from James Chapman on the extract from the official British 'propaganda' film, *Battle of the Somme*, which you have on your video:

> While the extract tells us nothing about the battle itself, we can see the effects of battle in the faces of soldiers on both sides, many of whom look dazed and confused. While some men look at the camera, there is nothing

like the waving and cheering that characterized the newsreels of 1914. The pictures of both British and German wounded give some indication of the common experience of warfare. There does not appear to be any antagonism between the British and German soldiers: you may have noted one scene in which a British soldier is handing out cigarettes to the prisoners (though the line of men standing in the background watching this act suggests that it may have been staged for the camera). Interestingly, given that so many of our impressions of the Somme are of men falling down in the mud, this extract shows the ground to be hard, and the weather hot and dusty (note the number of men in shirt-sleeves).

(Units 7–10, p.186)

Probably the clutch of films of most value to historians interested in a concrete historical topic, apart from propaganda, is that discussed by Tony Aldgate and James Chapman in Book 4, Units 21–25, section 3, which is concerned with the debate over whether or not the Second World War resulted in positive social reform. Notice that all of them are confined to the possibly exceptional case of Britain, the German films discussed being obviously concerned with other matters. Tony Aldgate and James Chapman give a number of examples of both feature films and documentary films. These films (wittingly or unwittingly) bring out the important roles of women in wartime – most notable, of course, is the 1943 feature film *Millions Like Us*. Tony Aldgate and James Chapman discuss the *radio* broadcasts of novelist J. B. Priestley as being 'propagandist' in the sense of being aimed at boosting morale, but the broadcasts also contain social reform messages:

Priestley believes there can be no going back to 'the old days'. The war has brought about social and economic changes in British society and the only thing to do is to capitalize on them with the aim of producing a new and better order.

(Units 21–25, p.181)

Returning to films, they continue:

The two films you have just watched echo the same themes evident in Priestley's 'new world order' broadcasts. Roy Boulting's *The Dawn Guard* (released to cinemas in January 1941 and the non-theatrical circuit in March 1941) and Gilbert Gunn's *Tyneside Story* (given a non-theatrical release in January 1944 but not released to cinemas) harp upon the idea of war as 'the midwife of social progress'. Both vividly contrast 'the bad days' of the 1930s, with the potentially beneficial changes wrought by war, and argue that these should point the way to a better planned, more rational, fair-minded and equitable society in the future.

(Units 21–25, p.182)

As you would expect, the evidence provided by the British media and sources such as the films and broadcasts you have examined, does not provide an easy or obvious answer to the overarching question of whether war brought about social change, any more than does the evidence put forward by other historians in the debate. But it does bear eloquent witness, I am sure you will agree, to the fact that many people felt profound changes were afoot in society, born largely of the country's wartime experiences, and that these changes could prove beneficial. It also provides abundant evidence of the desire and commitment to built 'a better world' once the war had been won.

Exercise   With regard to the question of whether the war experience brought social change or not, what is the biggest single deficiency in this film evidence? ∎

Specimen answer   While it tells us about changing attitudes *during* the war, it does not tell us what actually happened after the war. I hope you got that one: it is a point to be constantly borne in mind when reflecting on some of the major issues of our course. □

But now to art and music (and I shall concentrate on the difficult spheres of élite art and music). If we say that the important changes of war are those that affected the largest numbers of people, we can argue that these are more likely to be evidenced or responded to in the more popular arts, such as film. However, we could also argue that the really profound changes of war, those that affected the mind and spirit of humanity, are more likely to be seen in the 'higher' art forms. Perhaps the most balanced thing to say is that one type of change is best seen in one type of cultural artefact, and the other type of change is best seen in the other type of cultural artefact. The horrific impact of the First World War, the way it turned optimism and idealism to cynicism and despair, is clearly shown in the selection of paintings we have given you in the *Audio Art Pack*. Just consider the words of the futurists, and look at the Giacomo Balla painting; consider the words and actions of the British futurist (or Vorticist) C. R. W. Nevinson, and look at the 1914 painting by Otto Dix; then look at Nevinson's *La Mitrailleuse* of 1915, and the pictures by Max Beckmann, Otto Dix and Max Ernst, which were painted at the end of the war.

With music it is less clear-cut. Elgar's *The Spirit of England* may suggest the impact of war as creating a kind of elegiac celebration of heroism but certainly not triumphalism (such as one might associate with the pre-war *Pomp and Circumstance* marches). The *Concerto in D for the Left Hand* was specially written by Ravel for a one-armed ex-soldier – that in a sense speaks for itself. A note of deep tragedy certainly entered Ravel's work during and after the war: critics are divided as to whether this is the key mood of the concerto, or whether the mood is rather one of mocking cynicism. With regard to the Second World War, Shostakovich's *Leningrad Symphony* is certainly highly symbolic, signifying resistance to Nazi Germany and the unity in that cause between the western Allies and Soviet Russia. The Britten *War Requiem* speaks of the reconciliation (one might almost say 'union') engendered at the end of the Second World War. These are very encapsulated comments because, if you are going to attempt questions on art and music, you really do have to remind yourself of the detailed comments on the audios. I leave to the next sub-section questions about using art and music as sources from which to analyse the effects of war on art and music themselves.

The effects of war on the arts, film and radio

It is a good idea to look first at the technological aspects. The great increase in the capacity to produce radio valves was an important influence in the development of broadcasting in the post-war years, and thus, indirectly, on the expansion of classical music. In the Second World War, as explained in detail in Units 21–25, section 3, there was a crucial development, entirely related to the needs of war, in the production of high-quality gramophone records, again with a spin-off effect on music. The big change in film technology (sound) came in the interwar years and is not related to the war.

However, as Tony Aldgate and James Chapman bring out, the war did have important effects in:

1   bringing great prestige to film and increasing its acceptability among the middle and upper classes;

2   making film a 'national' rather than an 'international' medium, with the development of distinct and powerful cinema traditions in the different European countries; it also, however, created a completely new ascendancy for American films, against which European companies had constantly to struggle.

Film in the interwar years is undoubtedly much more sophisticated than it had been in the pre-war years. With the advent of sound, newsreels become a most important medium for communicating 'news' (often rather trivial) to the masses – more important at this time than radio, though the many uses of radio during the Second World War turn it into the most important news medium (reflect for a moment on Richard Dimbleby's concentration camp report). As section 3 shows, feature films (ostensibly directed at entertainment) very much become part of the war effort in Germany and Britain. They gain further in both prestige and audiences, and after the war they are the most important medium for *entertainment* (radio being the most important *news* medium). However, radio also had an entertainment function; section 3 shows how, in 'the people's war', the BBC, perhaps slightly reluctantly, did lighten its offerings, as seen, for instance, in *ITMA* and *Workers' Playtime*.

As ever, working out the effects of the wars on art and music is still more complex. In the course materials, and in the two articles by me supplied at Residential School, a constant theme is that we have to distinguish between the effects of war on the individual paintings, or even on the general style, of individual artists, and the effects of war on the whole language of art or music, or on movements (for example, neo-classicism in music, or surrealism in art). As you know (and make sure this comes through in anything you write), modernism in both art and music was already firmly established well before the First World War. However, it is argued that Dada can be seen very much as a direct response to the war, and that Dada, allied to other developments, such as the study of the psychological damage suffered by soldiers, led to surrealism as the major movement of the interwar years. You do not have to agree with this thesis, and if you do agree with it you must support it with much detailed evidence. Just stating the thesis is not enough. With regard to the Second World War and Europe there is not such a firm statement to be made. The new movement is abstract expressionism, but that developed in America. The nearest equivalent in Europe is *art informel*, whose development is traced in the audio through the work of Jean Fautrier.

The impact of the war on Fautrier *as an individual* is seen in his particular mode of incorporating tiny human faces in the great blobs of paint of which his paintings are made up. Similarly, Beckmann's reactions to the First World War (though his work is subsequently much imitated) are highly personal. It is for you to work out, with the appropriate evidence, how you establish the balance between purely personal reactions and the question of how art in general was affected by the wars. But do show that you are at least aware of the distinction. Just listing painters and paintings and how the war seems to show up in their works just won't do. There seems to be some kind of law (but as there are no laws in history, just call this a thesis!) that music reacts more slowly to historical change than any of the other art forms. I don't think we can detect any great change in musical language over the period of the First World War (remember pre-war Stravinsky), though you might have picked up from your Residential School reading the example of the neo-classicism in music principally developed by this same Stravinsky (*The Rite of Spring* is very definitely not classical in any sense!). The suggestion in the audio, however, is that the Second World War did bring a very complete break, represented in particular by the avant-garde music of Pierre Boulez. What is also suggested, with respect to both art and music, is that the First World War, in all its horror and catastrophe, did make the modes of modernism more acceptable to wider audiences; or at least it familiarized people with the idea that modernist art and modernist music represented this modern age.

The wars, one could argue, changed the relationships between the arts and their audiences; perhaps they also changed relationships between the arts and governments. All of this can be tied up with my own arguments about the significance of the First World War in the development of mass society. Again you would need to check what is said on the audio, in the course material, and in the extra Residential School reading: there is no point unloading generalizations if you can't give supporting evidence. All the evidence we have provided you with comes from Britain. In both wars governments set up official war artists: despite his disenchanted view of the First World War, Nevinson became one at the end of that war (as did an equally disenchanted artist, Paul Nash). Stanley Spencer was an official war artist in both wars: his paintings of Clyde shipbuilders are very revealing with respect to the effects of the Second World War on social reform. Indeed, you could use them as evidence along with the clutch of films cited in Units 21–25, section 3, which I have already mentioned.

Which of the two wars had the greater effect on the arts?

I have nothing to add to what I have already said about radio and film. From what I have said about art, the implication is that the First World War had the greater effect. With regard to music, however, if we take into account Boulez and his school, the Second World War had the greater effect. (Other kinds of classical music continued, of course – for example, the music of Britten.)

I insert this short discussion here, because the questions you are likely to be asked will probably feature total war in general, rather than one or other of the two wars. Nonetheless, you may well find it useful (breaking down the question into its components once more) to separate out the First World War from the Second World War, rather than to plunge in and make generalizations about the two wars taken together. However, if you simply said 'the First World War did this, and the Second World War did that', your answer would in most cases be incomplete. In the end, as always in this kind of topic, we are interested in your overall evaluation of the significance of war, as against other factors.

Propaganda

If I were asked the question: 'Which is more effective as a propaganda medium, film or painting?', I think the answer 'film' would be practically unchallengeable. I would go so far as to say that any painting that is propagandist is not really art – though obviously certain forms of popular art, posters and cartoons say, can be very propagandist in nature. In this sub-section I will concentrate almost exclusively on film and radio, though I will make a few comments about art and music at the end.

In discussing film and radio that is held to be propagandist, it is always worthwhile starting off by asking who is responsible for the particular film or radio programme, and what cause is it advocating. In Units 21–25, section 3, Tony Aldgate and James Chapman distinguish between propaganda items made by governments, on behalf of the government and (allegedly) the nation, and propaganda items made on behalf of individual (usually political) causes. They identify Hitler's *Mein Kampf* as an example of the latter. German newsreels in the Hitler period were so much subject to government influence and control that they were effectively government propaganda. The situation of British newsreels in the same period is slightly different, but in general they are happy to support government policies, and in particular a Conservative (nominally 'National') government with which they closely identify. The great Russian film-makers of the 1920s discussed by Tony Aldgate in Book 3, Unit 18 are nominally independent directors, but in fact they identify themselves wholly with the aims and ethos of the Soviet regime, and are eager to show how this wonderful new medium, film, can be used to advance what they see as a noble cause. Incidentally, in all this, we may have a good indication of a classic difference between totalitarian regimes and liberal democratic ones. Whatever the nominal situation, films made in the former very much conform to what the relevant government would wish to have said; in liberal democratic Britain, while the newsreel companies generally share the outlook of the government, they are able (as Tony Aldgate and James Chapman show) to demonstrate occasional elements of independence.

You might well be asked to discuss comparisons and contrasts between the propaganda efforts and achievements of Britain, Russia and Germany. It does have to be recognized that, because of the need to go into some detail with regard to the film extracts that we have been able to obtain for the videos, our coverage of different countries is very patchy. In Book 2, Units 7–10, section 3, James Chapman gives an excellent overview of First World War developments in many different European countries (it is well worth rereading this now), but when it comes to propaganda he (very properly) concentrates on the extracts from *British* films on your video. In Book 3, Unit 18, Tony Aldgate gives an illuminating account of the use made of feature films in the Soviet Union to propagate (through highly sophisticated use of film techniques) the ideals of Soviet Communism: this, however, is essentially confined to the 1920s. He then makes direct comparisons between Germany and Britain in the 1930s. In Book 4, Units 21–25, for the Second World War, Tony Aldgate and James Chapman again make direct comparisons between Britain and Germany. In any exam answer it would be wise to explain at the outset that the nature of your own coverage will necessarily be limited by the resources you have been provided with in the course. In what follows, I shall closely follow the course material in discussing four topics:

1   British propaganda in the First World War;

2   Soviet feature films;

3   German and British propaganda in the interwar years;

4   German and British propaganda in the Second World War, together with some comments on British/American propaganda in post-war Germany. Discussing British propaganda in the Second World War brings out the many uses to which propaganda was put: apart from justifying the country's cause both abroad and at home, attention had to be paid to domestic morale, publicizing and explaining various domestic policies (such as rationing), encouraging people (and most directly, of course, housewives) to use scarce food and other commodities economically and wisely, and recruiting women for war work. All but the first of these perhaps deserve almost to be regarded as communication and information as much as propaganda. With that thought in mind, we might ask ourselves whether *all* propaganda is inevitably dishonest, or just certain kinds of propaganda; whether the faking of information and evidence is inevitable; whether it is possible to be broadly propagandist and yet at the same time honest.

British propaganda in the First World War

James Chapman tells us that the twenty-seven short films released during the first six months of 1916 were disappointing, failing to give any serious impression of the realities of the war, and were ineffective as propaganda. Things changed with *Battle of the Somme*, released in August 1916, which 'made an enormous impact on the British public' (Units 7–10, p.185). I've already given you his comments on some of the unwitting testimony contained in the film. Here is an interesting revelation of one of its propaganda elements:

> The most interesting thing about the extract to my mind, however, is the inter-title at the beginning which states: 'British Wounded and Nerve-Shattered German Prisoners Arriving'. We know that the British army long wanted to deny that 'shell shock' was a real medical condition. The implication of this inter-title is that British soldiers do not suffer from shell shock but that German soldiers do. This is an example of propaganda, intended to create the impression for audiences at home that the Germans' ability and will to fight was being destroyed – which, as we know, was very far from the truth in 1916.

(Units 7–10, p.186)

James Chapman does point out that a certain amount of material, not surprisingly, was faked, but that this is reckoned to be rather small in proportion to the complete work.

Soviet feature films

Tony Aldgate refers to Roberts in stating that:

> the cinema was especially valuable in a country with a mainly illiterate population. All the Bolshevik leaders testified to its significance. Lenin commented that 'of all the arts for us the cinema is the most important'; Stalin called it 'the greatest means of mass agitation'; and Trotsky considered it 'the best instrument for propaganda'. Anatoli Lunacharsky, the People's Commissar for Enlightenment, set out 'The tasks of the state cinema in the RSFSR' in 1919, which you will find as Document 1.13 in *Primary Sources 2: Interwar and World War II*. Its major purpose, he stated, was to reach 'the mind and the heart' of the people with 'revolutionary propaganda'.

(Unit 18, p.8)

He mentions Eisenstein's trilogy of films, including *Battleship Potemkin* (1926), about a revolutionary incident in 1905, and *October* (1927), which celebrates the 1917 revolution, together with Podovkin's *Mother* (1926) and *The End of St Petersburg* (1927), and Dovzhenko's *Arsenal* (1929), all of which, he says, 'amply chronicled the development of revolutionary consciousness' (Unit 18, p.9).

It seemed that these films were miracles of propaganda, resulting in them being banned from public exhibition in Britain and France (their great reputation was acquired through their being shown in private clubs and societies). Despite attempted bans, *Potemkin* was released in 150 cinemas and proved a popular success. But Tony Aldgate concludes that despite this mighty reputation abroad, the films were not really successful at home, and were not being watched 'by the people for whom they were primarily intended' – the masses.

German and British propaganda in the interwar years

As Tony Aldgate puts it, for an effective example of Hitler's propaganda once the National Socialists had assumed power in 1933, 'one need only look at the film of the 1934 Party rally in Nuremberg, which was made "by order of the Führer" and released with the title of the theme of the rally, *Triumph of the Will* (*Triumph des Willens*)' (Unit 18, p.11). Item 23 on Video 1 is a sequence from *Triumph of the Will*. Here is part of the commentary on that sequence by film critic Richard Meran Barsam:

> The stage and the podium are constructed to place Hitler apart from his immediate entourage and, more important, high above the crowd. Here the people are reduced to architectural patterns, deprived of their individuality in favour of some larger communal ideal. This is accomplished through the use of flags, as if they were costumes, to cover the participants and through the distorted visual effects created by a telephoto lens. This reduction of people into masses is juxtaposed to an equally distorted elevation of the *Führer* ... From this point on, Riefenstahl [the female film-maker usually credited with directing and editing the film] continues to develop the godlike presence that began with motif and music in the early moments of the film. Now the controlling images are the recurrent shots of the huge architectural eagle and swastika and, of course, the forest of flags. Now

while the canvas is crowded to the borders with men, we are given a clear picture of only one of them; the rest are supporting characters, faceless and unidentified ...

Moving from its position on tracks below and to the side of the high podium, the camera records Hitler's speech in a series of shots looking up at him, shots from behind, and close-ups, medium and long shots. These shots are intercut with shots of the faces of the listening audience of flag-bearers.

(Richard Meran Barsam, *Filmguide to 'Triumph of the Will'*, 1975, pp.49–52)

I have quoted this at length to give an example of what a really detailed, critical commentary on a film looks like.

Obviously we can't expect you to produce anything quite like that in an exam. But it is important, when talking about film, to give some sense of what actually is in the film and of the production techniques deployed. Making relevant, telling, critical points about films you have studied (and making relevant, telling, critical points about paintings you have looked at and music you have listened to) is as much a part of the historical training provided by this course as doing the same things for more traditional written documents. Note that critical discussion of a film (or a novel for that matter) is not the same as telling the story in detail. We don't want tedious plot summaries, but rather relevant comments on specific points.

For radio in the interwar years we have detailed discussion only for Britain, though Tony Aldgate does note that radio was an ideal instrument of propaganda, greatly used in both Russia and Germany. He notes that of the thirty European national broadcasting systems in existence in 1938, thirteen were state owned and run, nine were government monopolies, four were directly operated by governments, and only three were privately owned (Unit 18, p.15). The BBC, a government monopoly (technically, a 'public corporation'), operating with a 'measure of autonomy and independence', to quite lofty aims, was widely recognized as a model institution.

Tony Aldgate gives a very balanced account of the relationships between the BBC and the government, a test case being provided by the BBC's coverage of the General Strike of 3 May to 12 May 1926: there was no fabrication or distortion, but the points of view of the TUC and the miners were simply not reported.

You have a range of fascinating material on Audio 3. Note this comment on the treatment of 'The Battle of Cable Street' in item 9, 'Radio Gazette No. 1 – review of events at home and abroad' (10 October 1936):

Notice, also, the commentator's emphasis upon 'the crowd' and 'the mob' which gets out of hand only to be put firmly in its place by the valiant 'cops'. The report, in short, ends up as a fulsome tribute to the British police and the events are presented solely as a matter relating to the question of 'law and order' – an interpretation which was reinforced constantly in many a newsreel story of the day, regardless of the event being covered.

(Unit 18, p.22)

Note the reference to newsreels. I think it would generally be fair to say that the newsreels, though privately owned, very much adopt the same stance as the BBC. Tony Aldgate points out that while Gaumont British News claimed to be 'non-party' it managed to present Prime Minister Stanley Baldwin

(Conservative), in a much more favourable light than Leader of the Opposition Clement Attlee (Labour). Note with regard to items 20, 25, 26, 27 and 29, that the newsreels were giving support to rearmament.

German and British propaganda in the Second World War

It seems that, at the start of the war, Germany was far ahead of Britain in the 'art' of propaganda (though perhaps by the end of the war the relatively low-key, understated, British propaganda was proving to be more effective – decide for yourself).

On Video 2 you have three extracts from the 1941 feature film *Ohm Kruger* (*Uncle Kruger*) (items 11–13) and one extract from the 1940 film *Der Ewige Jude* (*The Eternal/Wandering Jew*) (item 14). *Der Ewige Jude* is documentary in style (with some excerpts from feature film), though I think we would have to say that it is a highly perverted kind of 'documentary'. *Ohm Kruger*, set in the Boer War, is straight anti-British propaganda, aimed at Germany's domestic population and intended to strengthen their determination to wage war against the wicked British. Was it effective as propaganda?

> The security service (SD) summary of audience reactions to the film gives you a better idea of how it was received in its day ... Apart from the inevitable reservations about occasional scenes being 'too heavily loaded' with propagandist intent, the film does appear to have been a considerable success. It seems also to have genuinely fulfilled its function in helping to stiffen anti-British sentiment and resolve.
>
> (Units 21–25, p.171)

It seems that after great initial success *Der Ewige Jude* lost much of its appeal for German audiences:

> Consequently, and unsurprisingly, *Der Ewige Jude* was dubbed and distributed to all Nazi-occupied countries. It attracted very large audiences, not least in France, where free exhibitions ensured its success despite the proven popularity, once again, of *Jud Süss*. Furthermore, a specially edited and adapted French version was released ten days before the round-up of some 13,000 Jews in preparation for their mass deportation to the east. The film was clearly intended to prepare public opinion for such an event, and it is in this regard that the importance of such films to the Nazi regime can be seen.
>
> (Units 21–25, p.175)

I have already referred to some of the British documentary items dealing with life on the home front and issues of social reform. Two major feature films of great significance are *The Gentle Sex* and *Millions Like Us*. Both films, and the extracts from them you have on Video 2 as items 5 and 6, are discussed by me at the end of the sub-section 'Women in British wartime films' in Units 21–25, section 2 (pp.142–4). The Ministry of Information 'shorts' (such as *Miss Grant Goes to the Door*, released in August 1940, and included on Video 2 as item 15) are short fiction films. *London Can Take It*, made for distribution in the United States, then in a shorter version, as *Britain Can Take It*, is documentary in style:

> Directed by Harry Watt and Humphrey Jennings, with a commentary written and narrated by Quentin Reynolds, the London war correspondent for the

US magazine *Collier's Weekly*, it was released to cinemas in October 1940 and put on the non-theatrical circuit in December 1940. It was made in two versions: a five-minute film for domestic consumption ... and a longer version ... for exhibition in the US under the title *London Can Take It* and with a running time of ten minutes. Its theme is expressed in the latter title, suggested by Reynolds, and its story is of London in the Blitz. The story is related in a deadpan and underplayed style, with the emphasis on a seemingly straightforward and factual narration of events. It is not dramatized at all, nor does it use actors; it was plainly intended as a piece of descriptive reportage and was meant to convey the impression, 'this is how it is in wartime London'.

'These are not Hollywood sound effects', Reynolds points out as he proceeds to show the devastation caused by 'the nightly siege of London' ... there is repeated reference to the moulding of a new 'people's army' and to the high morale of the population despite its tribulations. The film was greeted with much critical acclaim in Britain.

(Units 21–25, pp.179–80)

Among the British public, *Britain Can Take It* topped a popularity poll of official films. Cunningly, all British credits were removed from the film for its showing in America: 'Once more, it proved to be immensely popular' (Units 21–25, p.180).

Some brief thoughts on the 'Britain versus Germany' question. 'Nazi propaganda', Tony Aldgate and James Chapman tell us, 'definitely scored some notable successes'. Yet they also suggest that: 'It may be, indeed, that Nazi propaganda had reached its peak by 1939' (Units 21–25, p.190). Britain seems to be winning the propaganda war. But note their reservations on the second story of item 18 on Video 2 – Field Marshal Montgomery talking to factory workers:

Again, you will doubtless note, there is the same sense of the proceedings being well orchestrated, with the appropriate amount of careful editing to convey a feeling of 'spontaneous' rapport between 'Monty' and everyday folk. Despite the editing, however, some things cannot be hidden. Notice the distinctly autocratic air and the patriarchal tone. Monty and the workers ('and women too') were one 'big happy family', yet they remained classes apart.

(Units 21–25, p.192)

(The 'Monty' film, of course, is important with regard to our earlier discussions of social unity and expected social reform.)

Tony Aldgate and James Chapman's discussion of the propaganda uses of film concludes with some remarks on the Allies' attempts to 're-educate' Germans after the war. These, they believe, were not particularly successful.

Are the powers of propaganda, in fact, overstated? Is propaganda only really effective to the extent that the cause being advocated is a good one? Don't the 'masses', at whom most propaganda is aimed, quite quickly react against it? Aren't films at their best when they are entertainment, or art? With regard to art and music, it is worth remembering that *Guernica* became a great symbol of Nazi cruelty, the *Leningrad Symphony* a great symbol of the Soviet–western alliance against Hitler, and that support for modern art and music (which Hitler condemned as 'decadent') came to be represented as part of the great battle against Nazi evil and obscurantism. And Stravinsky and Boulez obviously saw the fuss surrounding the *War Requiem* as a kind of British jingoism.

6 CONCLUSION

We all hope that this book has been genuinely useful to you in helping you to reflect on what you have learned throughout the year, and thus help you to prepare for the exam. Of course, you will also have had advice from your own tutor. This is the appropriate moment to pay tribute to our Associate Lecturers, upon whom we depend greatly for the success of the whole enterprise. You as a student have a part to play as well. Students and Associate Lecturers came together in giving us advice on our predecessor course, A813, and in planning and writing AA312 we have responded very positively to all the different kinds of feedback we received.

We are aware that there is a great amount of very rich material in AA312, but we do believe the workloads involved are fair ones. We have also made great efforts to ensure that throughout the course the work is evenly spread, and carefully paced. Two wishes are now uppermost in our minds:

1   that you have enjoyed the course and profited greatly from it;

2   that you will now successfully display what you have learned in the exam.

References

Addison, P. (1975) *The Road to 1945: British Politics and the Second World War*, Jonathan Cape.

Arendt, H. (1963) *On Revolution*, Penguin.

Barsam, R. M. (1975) *Filmguide to 'Triumph of the Will'*, Indiana University Press.

Bartov, O. (1985) *The Eastern Front 1941–1945: German Troops and the Barbarisation of Warfare*, Macmillan in association with St Anthony's College, Oxford.

Bessel, R. (1993) *Germany after the First World War*, Clarendon Press.

Bourke, J. (1996) *Dismembering the Male: Men's Bodies, Britain and the Great War*, Reaktion Books.

Bourke, J. (1999) *An Intimate History of Killing: Face-to-Face Killing in Twentieth-Century Warfare*, Granta.

Chickering, R. (1998) *Imperial Germany and the Great War, 1914–1918*, Cambridge University Press.

Clark, M. (1984) *Modern Italy 1871–1982*, Longman.

Daniel, U. (1988) 'Women's work in industry and family: Germany 1914–1918', in R. Wall and J. Winter (eds) *The Upheaval of War: Family, Work and Welfare in Europe, 1914–1918*, Cambridge University Press.

Daniel, U. (1997) *The War from Within: German Working-Class Women in the First World War*, Berg.

de Grazia, V. (1992) *How Fascism Ruled Women: Italy, 1922–1945*, University of California Press.

Gagnon, P. (1972) *France since 1789*, Harper and Row.

Hause, S. C. (1987) 'More Minerva than Mars: the French Women's Rights Campaign and the First World War', in M. R. Higonnet, J. Jenson, S. Michel and M. C. Weitz (eds) *Behind the Lines: Gender and the Two World Wars*, Yale University Press.

Herwig, H. H. (1997) *The First World War: Germany and Austria-Hungary 1914–1918*, Arnold.

Howard, M. (1976) 'Total war in the twentieth century: participation and consensus in the Second World War', in Brian Bond and Ian Roy (eds) *War and Society: A Yearbook of Military History*, Croom Helm.

Jefferys, K. (1991) *The Churchill Coalition and Wartime Politics 1940–1945*, Manchester University Press.

Kedward, H. R. (1993) *In Search of the Maquis: Rural Resistance in Southern France 1942–1944*, Clarendon Press.

Kent, S. K. (1988) 'The politics of sexual difference: World War One and the demise of British feminism', *Journal of British Studies*, vol.27, no.3, pp.232–53.

Kent, S. K. (1993) *Making Peace: The Reconstruction of Gender in Interwar Britain*, Princeton University Press.

Levine, P. (1993) 'Rough usage: prostitution, law and the social historian', in A. Wilson (ed.) *Rethinking Social History: English Society 1570–1920 and its Interpretation*, Manchester University Press.

Marwick, A. (1965) *The Deluge: British Society and the First World War*, Macmillan.

Marwick, A. (1974) *War and Social Change in the Twentieth Century*, London, Macmillan.

Marwick, A. (1988) *Total War and Social Change*, Macmillan.

McKibbin, R. (1974) *The Evolution of the Labour Party, 1910–1920*, Clarendon Press.

McKibbin, R. (1990) *The Ideologies of Class: Social Relations in Britain 1880–1950*, Clarendon Press.

Noakes, J. (1992) 'Germany', in J. Noakes (ed.) *The Civilian in War: The Home Front in Europe, Japan and the USA in World War II*, University of Exeter Press.

O'Brien, C. (1996) 'Beyond the can[n]on: French women's responses to the First World War', *French Cultural Studies*, vol.7, no.20, pp.201–13.

Perrot, M. (1987) 'The New Eve and the Old Adam: changes in French women's condition at the turn of the century', in M. R. Higonnet, J. Jenson, S. Michel and M. C. Weitz (eds) *Behind the Lines: Gender and the Two World Wars*, Yale University Press.

Pugh, M. (1992) *Women and the Women's Movement in Britain, 1914–1959*, Macmillan.

Reid, A. (1988) 'World War I and the working class in Britain', in A. Marwick (ed.) *Total War and Social Change*, Macmillan.

Smith, H. L. (1986) 'The effect of war on the status of women', in H. L. Smith (ed.) *War and Social Change. British Society in the Second World War*, Manchester University Press.

Summerfield, P. (1989) *Women Workers in the Second World War: Production and Patriarchy in Conflict*, 2nd edn, Routledge.

Summerfield, P. (1998) *Reconstructing Women's Wartime Lives: Discourse and Subjectivity in Oral Histories of the Second World War*, Manchester University Press.

Wall, R. and Winter, J. (1988) *The Upheaval of War: Family, Work and Welfare in Europe 1914–1918*, Cambridge University Press.

Welch, D. (1983) *Propaganda and the German Cinema 1933–1945*, Clarendon Press.

Index